Scottish

Castles

& Fortifications

Richard Dargie

Scottish Castles
& Fortifications

Author - Richard Lewis Campbell Dargie

Photography - Graeme & Derek Wallace

Design - Kevin Jeffery

Reprographics - GWP Graphics

Printing - Printer Trento

Published by

GW Publishing

PO Box 6091

Thatcham

Berks

RG19 8XZ

Tel +44 (0) 1635 268080

First Published 2004

Copyright GW Publishing

ISBN 0 9546701 1 6

Publishing

www.gwpublishing.com

⊰⊱ Contents ⊰⊱

Geology has given Scotland thousands of places fit for castles, while history has ensured that the peoples of Scotland have had to fortify their land to an unparalleled extent. Consequently, Scotland still bristles with forts and keeps and tower houses even to this day. A glance at a map of any part of Scotland reveals just how many fortresses have been built upon this land. Most have now vanished, cast down by the weather and cannibalised by later builders. Many have left only a faint impression on the contours of the landscape, or an old half-forgotten place name. Yet thousands of impressive strongholds from Scotland's long and bloodied past still survive. This book celebrates over one hundred of the finest of them.

Scotland's strongholds evolved over time as political conditions changed and as the needs of the Scottish people developed. Brochs, duns, peels and crannogs were used for defence for millennia. Strong walls were needed in the brutal Dark Age wars of Dalriada, Alba, Pictland and Strathclyde. Natural fortresses such as Edinburgh and Dumbarton were understandably amongst the earliest defended sites in recorded times. However, the building of the first true castles coincides with the founding of a new Scottish kingdom in the eleventh and twelfth centuries when Scotland looked to feudal Europe more than to its Celtic past.

The conquest and enslavement of the English by the Norman French after 1066 was the spur to change in Scotland. The Scots soon realised that their new Norman neighbours possessed superior military technology and an effective social organization that made the most of available resources. Malcolm Canmore was quick to treat with William the Conqueror at Abernethy in 1072. Almost as quickly, Norman customs were imported into Scotland. Malcolm's openness to new ideas was symbolized by his marriage to Margaret, an intelligent women of Anglo-Hungarian descent who was familiar with the latest developments on the Continent. The first Norman style castle in Scotland was probably Malcolm's Tower in Dunfermline, now sadly reduced beyond recognition to a few low outcrops of stone. Within a generation, knights from Europe and England were settling in Scotland at the invitation of the King of Scots. These new landowners built timber forts on high mottes to look out on their estates. A classic example of this period in castle development survives at Duffus Castle; the resort of Freskin de Moravia, a Flemish or Norman adventurer given rich lands and privileges on the edge of the kingdom for as long as he could hold them with his sword. The age of castle building in Scotland had begun.

Time and increased wealth gave the opportunity to upgrade timber motte and bailey forts such as the Inverurie Bass to fireproof stone castles. The first of these were simple courtyards marked out by walls of enclosure as at Dunstaffnage and Castle Sween. Behind walls that were sixty feet high and ten feet thick were the lean-to sheds and halls where the castle folk lived and worked. By 1200 great stone keeps began to rise up within these castles of enceinte.

Yet many of the great stone castles of Scotland were not built where the modern visitor might expect them. The border with England always needed attention but the King of Scots had enemies enough in other directions. The Norse and their Gaelic allies held the West, Galloway was always rebellious and the mormaer earldoms of Ross and Moray saw little need to obey the king in distant Dunfermline. The first great castles such as Duffus and Rothesay were frontier outposts in long wars to win more territory for the kingdom. Highland fortresses such as Duart and Tioram seem remote today and the temptation is to imagine them as deliberately inaccessible bases where the clans could gather and plot their next raid undisturbed. However in the medieval and early modern periods, clan fortalices almost always controlled busy, profitable seaways and drove roads along which young cattle or stirks were taken toward market and the rich pastureland of the south.

There were always many different kinds of castle in medieval Scotland. Royal castles such as Stirling and Edinburgh were symbols of the king's authority. Other royal houses such as Falkland and Linlithgow were more private places of pleasure where the Stewarts could relax in safety. Great medieval bastions such as Hermitage and Dirleton that lay astride the roads from England had a function that was as much psychological as military. Most Scottish castles however were the homes and storehouses of local lords and the place where law and social order was maintained. Examples of these towers exist throughout Scotland and this book contains a representative example from different periods such as Borthwick, Smailholm and Claypotts. Other castles simply proclaimed that their owner had 'arrived'. The lawyer and historian John Scot of Scotstarvit had no real need of fortifications at his home near Cupar in Fife. Restoring his tower was a scholarly affectation and a sign of social distinction. No better example of this function of a castle exists than Craigievar in Aberdeenshire. Its soaring pinnacles tell all Strathdon that 'Danzig' Willie Forbes had made his mint in the Baltic trade. After 1700 new kinds of fortress reminded the Scots that they were now part of Hanoverian Britain. The barracks at Bernera and Ruthven were one sign of the British Government's determination to nullify the military threat from the Highlands. The vast scale of Fort George near Inverness, the largest fortifications built in eighteenth century Europe, indicates just how serious that threat was before the depopulation of northern Scotland.

Over time, as the kingdom prospered and the king's writ calmed the land, the need for defence gave way to the desire for luxury. Some castles had always been 'most pleasing' places to live as the charms of Edzell and Huntly testify. After 1680 however, many of the great families of Scotland had the wealth and the vision to build new palaces that fused older Scottish traditions with ideas from Europe as at Thirlstane and Drumlanrig. Thirlstane stands equal with any other great seventeenth century house on the Continent. With a classical core but fantastic decorations of a Caledonian stamp, Thirlestane fully proclaimed the status of the Duke of Lauderdale as the viceroy of the absent monarch in London. The 'Gothic' Inverary Castle performed the same function for the governors of western Scotland, the Campbell Dukes of Argyll. Castles were eventually rendered wholly obsolete by the social and economic changes that created modern Scotland. The last of the great tower houses, Leslie Castle in Aberdeenshire, was already effectively obsolete when it was erected in the 1660s. Yet long after the most remote Highlands glens had been pacified, something in the landscape encouraged patrons and architects to adorn new buildings with turrets in the Scots baronial style. Blair, Dunvegan and Dunrobin are only three of the many older castles that received a romantic Gothic or Scots baronial makeover in the nineteenth century long after the pacification of the Highlands. Castle building of a kind therefore continued well into the modern industrial age in Scotland, the kingdom of the castle.

This book is primarily concerned with explaining when and why the castles were built where they were. It aims to relate what is distinctive about their development and the lives and deeds of their owners, placing these within the wider context of Scottish history. It therefore concentrates on the few and usually relatively brief periods of conflict and struggle in Scottish history such as the war between the Scots and the Norse and Gaels in the mid-thirteenth century, the Wars for Scottish Independence between 1295 and 1339, the struggle between the Stewart kings and their over powerful Douglas vassals in the 1450s, the contest between Catholic pro-French and Protestant pro-English factions in Scotland in the 1550s, the periodic wars of the National Covenanting Revolution in the seventeenth century and the sporadic Jacobite risings between 1689 and 1746. This focus upon periods of political and military activity should not blind the reader to the fact that for most of their history, castles were centres of social, legal, economic and cultural activity during the long periods of relative calm and prosperity which medieval and early modern Scotland experienced.

200-1000	Picts, Scots, Britons and Angles build fortresses in Scotland using natural defensive features in the landscape.
870	Dumbarton Rock besieged by Vikings from Dublin under Olaf the White.
1100-1150	Construction of motte and bailey castles using earthworks and timber palisades such as the Bass at Inverurie or motte at Huntly.
1150s	Wars between the Norse & Gaels and the Normanised Kingdom of Scotland. Macdougall hegemony in the West.
1200-1250	Many original wooden castles upgraded into stone castles. Castles of enceinte or curtain wall built, especially in the contested lands in the west.
1260s	End of Norse presence in the western lands and islands.
1250-1300	Major development of towers, gatehouses and inner keeps at the great stone castles such as Caerlaverock, Rothesay, Dirleton, Hermitage and Kildrummy Castles.
1295-1356	Wars for Scottish Independence.
1295-1296	Most major Scottish castles taken and garrisoned by Edward I of England or by Scottish forces willing to collaborate with him.
1297-1298	William Wallace and Earl of Moray liberated many English-held castles especially after their victory at the Battle of Stirling Bridge.
1300-1305	Edward I systematically took main castles in Scotland beginning with siege of Caerlaverock.
1308	Robert the Bruce defeats the Comyns and slights their castles in the northeast.
1300-1329	The Bruce slights castles throughout Scotland so they cannot be used by invaders.
1309-1314	Recapture of remaining castles by Scots with Stirling Castle eventually liberated after the Battle of Bannockburn in 1314.
1332-1338	Edward III invades Scotland in support of his puppet king Edward Balliol. Many castles such as Dunbar badly damaged.
1350-1400	Evolution of first tower houses such as Clackmannan Tower.
1400-1450	Rise of noble power and development of baronial strongholds such as Doune, Threave and Tantallon castles. Castles in the west strengthened by Macdonald Lords of the Isles by adding central towers to curtain wall castles.
1450-1500	Stronger royal fortresses built, capable of giving and withstanding artillery fire such as Ravenscraig are built from scratch, while older castles such as Dunbar and Urquhart are modernised. Douglas strongholds such as Threave reduced.
1500-1550	Reinforcement of Stirling Castle by James IV and James V. Hamilton builds Craignethan Castle; an advanced artillery fortress.
1550-1575	Conflict between pro-French and pro-English factions in the Scottish elite spurs development of strategic artillery fortifications such as Broughty Castle.
1603	Union of the Crowns of Scotland and England.

1575-1600	Evolution of the developed tower house style such as at Claypotts Castle.
1600-1660	The great Castles of Mar (Crathes, Fraser, Fyvie,) evolve into their current form while the tower house reaches perfection at Craigievar. Last great tower house built at Leslie in Aberdeenshire.
1637	Outbreak of the National Revolution for the Covenant against the anglicising religious policies of Charles I.
1644-1645	Campaigns of the Marquis of Montrose and sack of Ballindalloch Castle.
1650-1652	Defeat of Scots Royalists at Worcester and Cromwellian invasion of Scotland.
1660-1715	First classical mansions built at Thirlstane, Drumlanrig & Floors.
1689	First Jacobite Rising by Bonnie Dundee in support of the Stewart dynasty.
1715	Earl of Mar raises Jacobite Standard at Braemar Castle.
1719	Spanish invasion of Glen Shiel and destruction of Eilean Donan Castle.
1746	Last castle siege in Britain at Blair Castle.
1750-1850	Castle fantasies built in Romantic Gothic and Scots Baronial styles evolve at sites such as Blair, Dunvegan, Inverary and Balmoral.
1810-1820	Worst phase of Highland Clearances on the Strathnaver estates of the Staffords, owners of Dunrobin Castle.
1847-1857	Balmoral Castle rebuilt by Victoria and Albert.

A note for non-Scottish readers:

Monarchs prior to the Union of the Crowns of 1603 are referred to by a numeral which represents their position in the Scottish royal lineage. Therefore James I refers to the fifteenth century Stewart King of Scots who reigned from 1406 to 1437. The designation James VI & I is used for the later Stewart monarch of both kingdoms who reigned in Scotland from 1567 and in England from 1603. The Scottish numeral precedes as Scotland is the older kingdom. The original Scottish spelling of Stewart, derived from stigeward or stye-warden but evolving into steward by 1200, is used throughout this book in preference to Stuart, the French form of the name used by Mary Queen of Scots as a result of her education at the French Court. Words which have a different meaning in Scotland than in England such as baron feature in the glossary, as do a number of Scots words used in the text. It should also be remembered that prior to the Union of 1707, the population of Scotland was far closer in size to that of England than has been the case subsequently. The relationship between the two kingdoms was therefore more one of equals than is the case today. The Highlands, virtually empty in the present age, were heavily populated prior to 1800 and were at different times an important source of well trained military manpower for recruiting sergeants from across Europe with Highlanders serving in the French, Swedish, Dutch, Polish, Russian and Ottoman armies. Scotland's historical significance should therefore not be judged by its current reduced condition.

Timeline of the monarchs and other key figures referred to in this book.

Donald II slain by Vikings at Dunnottar Castle in 895.

Constantine II (r.900-943) resisted the Vikings and survived siege of Dunnottar Castle.

Malcolm II (r.1005-34) defeated the Norse near Balvenie Castle in 1005.

Duncan I (r.1034-40) killed in battle by his former commander Macbeth near Elgin in 1040.

Macbeth (r.1040-57) one of the last Celtic or Alban Kings of the Scots, killed in battle by Malcolm III. Traditionally linked to Cawdor Castle in Morayshire.

Malcolm III (r.1058-93) the 'Canmore' or Great Chief who married (St) Margaret. A warrior king who strengthened Edinburgh Castle and his tower at Dunfermline.

David I (r.1124-53) gave feudal grants of land and rights to build castles to his Norman supporters such as Freskin of Duffus Castle.

William I (r. 1165-1214) the 'Lion' who fought the Norse in the West and the Celtic earls of Moray and Ross. Encouraged castle building in the Clyde valley as at Crookston Castle to hold these lands.

Alexander II (r.1214-49) quelled the revolt of the Celtic Moraymen in 1230 and established Castle Urquhart on Loch Ness.

Alexander III (r.1249-86) warrior king who defeated the Norse at the Battle of Largs in 1263 and carefully controlled vital strongholds in the West such as Skipness Castle.

Edward I of England (r.1272-1307) Longshanks, the warrior Plantagenet king who was known as the Hammer of the Scots.

John Balliol (r.1292-96) Chosen to reign when the Scottish royal house failed, he established the Auld Alliance between Scotland and France which sparked the invasion by Edward I of England in retaliation.

William Wallace (g.1296-99) Not king but Guardian of Scotland who defeated the English at Stirling Bridge in 1297 and briefly liberated castles throughout Scotland.

Robert I (r.1306-29) the Bruce who won back Scotland's castles from English hands and then slighted them so they could not be used by invaders again.

David II (r.1329-71) built a complex set of fortifications at Edinburgh Castle in 1361 known as King David's Tower.

Robert II (r.1371-90) the first Stewart monarch who spent much of his time on the family estates at Dundonald Castle in Ayrshire.

James I (r.1406-1437) Machiavellian monarch who cut his way to power through scheming relatives, establishing Linlithgow Palace as the Stewart royal home before being assassinated.

James II (r.1437-60) skilful king who destroyed the power of the Douglas clan and built Scotland's first artillery fortress at Ravenscraig Castle in Fife.

James III (r.1460-1488) ruthless centralising king whose plans to increase taxes and strengthen the military forces of the Crown upset the nobility and led to his death at the Battle of Sauchieburn.

James IV (r.1488-1513) successful Renaissance prince who greatly strengthened Stirling Castle before dying in battle at Flodden. James V (r.1513-1542) spent great revenues turning Linlithgow and Falkland into royal palaces of European stature.

Mary (r. 1542-67) Catholic monarch who tried to rule Protestant Scotland but was forced to abdicate at Lochleven Castle.

James VI & I (r.1567-1625) intelligent prince born in Edinburgh Castle who became King of England in 1603 and moved his Court to London in that year.

Charles I (r. 1625-1649) Crowned King of Scots in 1633, Charles' religious plans for Scotland sparked the great national Covenanting revolution that ultimately damaged many of Scotland's castles.

James Graham, Marquis of Montrose (1612-50) royalist general who won a series of victories against the Covenanters but was captured at the Battle of Carbisdale and executed in Edinburgh's Grassmarket.

Oliver Cromwell, Lord Protector of England from 1649-1658 who invaded Scotland and forced it into a Union with England in the 1650s. His troops destroyed numerous Scottish castles both deliberately and through accidental abuse.

Charles II (r. 1651-1685) Crowned at Scone in 1651, his army of Scottish supporters was defeated at Worcester shortly afterwards.

James VII & II (r.1685-1690) the last monarch to know Scotland well before Victoria, the Catholic James was removed from the throne by the Convention of 1689, sparking off the first Jacobite Rising.

John Graham of Claverhouse, Viscount Dundee (1648-89) known as Bonnie Dundee who died whilst winning a great victory for the Jacobite cause at Killiecrankie in 1689.

James Francis Stewart (1688-1766) the exiled Stewart prince recognised as James VIII & III in the Catholic courts of Europe and in Highland glens, nicknamed 'the Old Pretender'.

George I (r.1715-1727) the 'wee German lairdie' from Hanover whose accession sparked the 1715 Jacobite Rising.

Charles Edward Stewart (1720-88) Bonnie Prince Charlie, the Young Pretender who led the 1745 Rising in support of his father's right to the thrones of Scotland and England.

Victoria (r.1837-1901) established Balmoral Castle as the summer home of the British Royal Family in the 1840s.

The numbers on this map refer to the page numbers on page 4.

The First Fortresses

The first great strongholds in medieval Scotland took advantage of the country's unique geography. Volcanic rocks such as at Dumbarton were natural sites of refuge from which defenders could survey the surrounding countryside and look down upon their assailants. The profusion of rocks and promontories in Scotland's fragmented landscape that could be fortified impeded the forces of unification at work throughout other parts of Europe in the period. Dumbarton Castle is a reminder of the fact that well into the second Christian millennium, several kingdoms existed within the territory of present day Scotland. In the age before castles proper, Picts, Scots, Britons, Angles, Norse and Gallwegians all competed for space and resources in Caledonia. All of these separate peoples needed strongholds to protect themselves and their goods from their enemies. Many of these fortresses, such as the great Pictish fort at Burghead in Morayshire, vanished over time leaving few traces. Others such as Dumbarton were adapted for new purposes and survived into the later medieval age of castles.

Castle building in Scotland really began after 1124 when David I, King of Scots, invited the sons of Norman families to travel north and help him rule his kingdom. David had estates in England and had lived at the Norman court there. He had seen the energy of the Normans, then engaged in transforming the old tribal England that they had conquered into a powerful feudal state. David realized that the Normans offered the organization and military technology that he needed if his kingdom was to overcome its enemies. Norman knights who joined David were given lands and the right to build a castle. Everything and everyone on the new lord's states was to be directed towards feeding and equipping armed men for the service of the baron and the king. Not surprisingly, the lands granted to the Norman incomers were usually in disputed areas such as the Norse controlled western frontier or on the edge of the wild lands of Galloway where the King of Scot's writ did not always run.

The first Norman castles were motte and bailey structures similar to the chateau of Dol portrayed in the Bayeaux tapestry. The key fortification was the motte or earthen hill, surrounded by a palisade and surmounted by a wooden tower. An outer bailey or courtyard held stables, workshops and other services. Ramparts defended weak points such as gates and the whole complex was surrounded by a deep ditch or moat. The Bass at Inverurie is a classic surviving example of an early motte and bailey castle although other excellent examples survive at the Motte of Urr in the Stewartry and at Huntly. These castles served the new Norman barons well for several decades and were only gradually upgraded to stone versions in the 1200s. The classic instance of this transitional period in the development of Scottish castles is Duffus Castle in Morayshire. Duffus was originally a frontier base for the campaigns of Scottish kings against the unruly Celtic lords of Ross, Caithness and Sutherland. The replacement of its original wooden tower by a stone keep ended in disaster. The earthen motte gave way under the weight of the stone and the keep cracked open.

Castle Sween is another reminder of how precarious royal authority was in this period. Safe in their fortresses in the west, Highland lords such as the MacSweens and the MacDougalls could ignore edicts from the distant royal capital of Dunfermline with impugnity, choosing to side with the Norse in the thirteenth and the English in the fourteenth century. It took the deployment of massive resources such as those that went into the building of Rothesay Castle on Bute to bring the Norse and the western lords to heel.

The history of Scotland's castles is not just about conflict, war and siege however. In many parts of the land, the castle was a symbol of stability and continuity. One of the earliest Norman motte and bailey forts in Scotland, Aberdour Castle developed into a stone keep in the thirteenth century and was adapted into a fine baronial residence in the sixteenth. Until it was burned in 1688, Aberdour had enjoyed almost six centuries of peace and prosperity.

Dun Breatann, the 'fortress of the Britons' is the greatest Dark Age stronghold in these islands. A volcanic plug that dominates the Clyde basin, legend tells that St Patrick created this natural fortress when he hurled a rock at three pagan witches. Known in the old Celtic tongues as Alcluith, Dumbarton Rock has one of the longest recorded histories of any defensive site in Britain. British war bands and Pictish wizards feasted here listening to the great epic poem Gododdin. Merlin is said to have stayed here in 576 and in the Middle Ages Dumbarton was remembered as 'castrum arturi', the Camelot of Arthur and his chivalric court.

For almost five centuries Dumbarton Rock was capital of the independent kingdom of Strathclyde. Its darkest days came in 870 when the Norse king of Dublin Olaf the White laid seige for fifteen weeks. When the well spring high on the rock dried up, the weakened Britons were carried off in 200 longships to the slave markets in Ireland. The Rock only came to the King of Scots in 1018 after the Battle of Carham at the end of the long wars against Northumbria. Dumbarton then became a frontier outpost in Scotland's struggle with Norway for control of the Atlantic seaboard.

Dumbarton played a key strategic role in Scotland's victory over the Norse at nearby Largs in 1263. Edward Longshanks understood the Rock's importance and it was one of his first targets in the invasion of 1296. Edward's castellan at Dumbarton, John Stewart of Mentieth, captured Sir William Wallace in 1305 and legend says that the patriot was held in the Wallace Tower on the Rock before shipment to London for trial and dismemberment.

The massive Flemish bombard Mons Meg was fired against the Rock in 1489 when James IV twice laid seige to wrest the castle back from the rebellious Darnleys. In the turbulent years that followed the Reformation, Dumbarton Castle held out for Mary Queen of Scots. She was en route there when her forces were intercepted and routed in the skirmish at Langside near Glasgow. Her failure to reach 'safe Dumbarton' forced her to flee towards England and eventual execution. The Castle however was only taken back by the Protestants in 1571 when Thomas Crawford led his men up through the rocks and ramparts on the northern side of the Rock which had been thought impregnable. The Rock eventually served as a prison for defeated Jacobites awaiting transportation to the colonies.

David, Earl of Huntingdon, was one of the great magnates of twelfth and thirteenth century England, owning rich estates in the East Midlands and a fine castle at Fotheringay in Northamptonshire. David was also brother of Malcolm IV King of Scots and till 1198, was heir to the Scottish throne. As Earl of the Garioch in the north east of Scotland, his duty was to spread the Norman way of life into the old Celtic lands of Strathdon.

For this, David needed to build a castle and in the 1170s, he chose a point where the rivers Don and Urie meet in the heart of present day Aberdeenshire. Scholars disagree whether the great conical mound that still sits at that junction of waters is the result of geology or human action or both. What can be agreed is that the Bass of Inverurie is a massive, smoothly shaped structure that dominates the local landscape. Despite some levelling-down in the late 19th century, it remains almost 15 metres above the surrounding land. The fort's unusual name probably comes from the medieval Scots word for a workman's tool basket. Nearby, but now obscured by trees, stands the Little Bass that was once David's bailey where his men-at-arms could exercise and stable their horses.

The Bass was probably the first Norman style motte and bailey castle in the north east of Scotland. The timber fort was never replaced by a later stone structure, perhaps because the burgh of Inverurie that grew up around the fort was just far enough away from the higher lands that spawned rebels and raiders. The constables of the Bass, the Leslies, were to find themselves much busier upriver, protecting estates nearer the Highland passes.

David of Huntingdon was the great-great-grandfather of Robert the Bruce. In one of the strange ironies that mark Scottish history, a weary and dispirited Bruce rested for some weeks in the Bass fort at Inverurie at Christmas 1307 before venturing out to meet his Comyn rivals by nearby Barra Hill. Bruce's overwhelming success at the Battle of Barra marked the turning point in the war of liberation. Inevitably, a Donside cave a little upstream from the Bass is said to be where Bruce met his inspirational spider. It was however Bruce's policy to cast down and slight all strongholds that might be used against him and the Bass, as a fortress, disappears from historical view around this time.

Soldiers of fortune found a ready market for their skills in twelfth century Scotland, for the King of Scots had enemies on several fronts. In addition to Norman England in the south and the Norse in the west, there were problems in the north. Celtic-Pictish traditions were strong there, and loyalty was given to the local mormaer or earl rather than the distant king in Dunfermline toun. Moray was an especially troublesome border area between the old Celtic Alba and the new, emerging Scotto-Norman civilization. There were dangerous risings of the Moraymen in 1116 and 1130.

Enter Freskin, a mercenary knight from Flanders whose sword had already won him lands in West Lothian. He was exactly the kind of resourceful soldier that David I needed to impose the new feudal order upon Moray. David granted him the lands of Duffus on the Moray Firth and visited him in 1151 to inspect the fortifications that Freskin had built in order to hold his new estates.

Freskin erected the largest motte and earthwork castle in Scotland. He chose to build his timber keep upon a ridge of land with fine views across the marshy, low-lying 'laich o Moray'. For added safety he built up the surrounding earth and gravel to form an artificial mound and circled it with a deep boundary ditch. There were probably other watery defensive features, invisible today thanks to centuries of land reclamation by local farmers. Proud of the way that he had stamped himself upon the landscape, Freskin took the name de Moravia or Moray. His patriotic descendants were to prove stalwart defenders of Scotland's freedom.

By 1295 Freskin's wooden fortress had been replaced by a stone keep and the new castle was held by Sir Reginald de Chen or Cheyne. He paid homage to Edward I of England. Not surprisingly, national resistance to the English invasion erupted first in Moray. The lands of Duffus Castle were harried three times by patriot forces and Sir Reginald had to petition Edward for compensation. Duffus only passed back to the House of Freskin in 1350.

Douglases sacked the castle in 1452 and it was attacked by royalists under Montrose in 1645. Yet the greatest damage to Duffus Castle was done by the forces of nature. The twelfth century earthen motte was unequal to the weight of the later stone keep, which, at some unknown time in history, cracked and slipped downhill. Nevertheless, Duffus remains one of the great castles of early medieval Scotland.

Fleets of Norse longships, Gaelic birlinns and Catholic galleons have all attacked Castle Sween. This imposing structure above Loch Sween and the Sound of Jura is probably the oldest stone castle in Scotland and may have been built before 1100. The founder is thought to have been Suibhne (Sueno or Sven) of the O'Neills, one of the many warlords of the western seaboard who had a mixture of Gaelic, Irish and Norse blood coursing through his veins. Seapower was the key to controlling the broken coastline of western Scotland in the Middle Ages. With no deep harbourage nearby, the shallows beneath Castle Sween were perfect for beaching the shallow-draughted birlinns or war galleys used by medieval Highland chieftains.

Despite its remote location in lower Knapdale, and the Celtic origins of its first owners, the builders of Castle Sween understood the latest European fashions in military architecture. The castle has several Norman features including a doorway that closely resembles the portal of the Jew's House in Lincoln. The quadrangular walls were also strengthened by broad buttresses in the Norman style. From this redoubt, the sons of Suibhne, the MacSweens, built an extensive lordship in Argyll and Lorn.

Through loyalty to their Macdougall overlords, the MacSweens fought on the English side in the wars for Scottish independence. For this, they lost their lands when the English were defeated, and the castle was given by Bruce to his Macdonald allies. By 1450 Castle Sween was one of the pillars that supported the brilliant Macdonald Lordship of the Isles which threatened to overshadow the kingdom of Scotland in both military and cultural terms. Additional fifteenth century towers and the remains of a large barracks are evidence of the role that Castle Sween played in the Macdonald plan to establish a sovereign kingdom in the West.

When James IV finally smashed Macdonald power in 1493, loyal Colin Campbell, first Earl of Argyll, was given the task of keeping Castle Sween for the Crown. Castle Sween was still a Campbell stronghold when the wars of religion spread to Britain and Ireland in the 1640s. The Campbells were leaders of the Protestant Covenanting cause. Castle Sween was therefore a natural target for the Irish adventurer Alasdair MacColla who rampaged through Campbell Argyll on behalf of the royalist cause. In 1644 MacColla and his band of 1600 Irish gallowglass mercenaries, fresh from the Ulster massacres, attacked and destroyed the castle. It has been a ruin ever since.

Magnus Barelegs, King of Norway, Hebrides and Man built the first wooden castle at Rothesay around 1098, for the island of Bute, though barely thirty miles from Glasgow, belonged to the Norsemen for much of the Middle Ages. Bute only became part of the Scottish kingdom around 1200 when William the Lion seized control of the Firth of Clyde. The construction of the magnificent castle that now stands upon Bareleg's mound was probably begun by Walter, Heriditary Steward of the King of Scots, soon after that date. Walter's stone shell keep is still surrounded by the wet moat fed by a burn from Loch Fad.

Rothesay was soon back in Viking hands. The saga of Haakon Haakonson tells how Uspak King of Man and the Isles beseiged the Scots in Rothesay for three days in 1230. The defenders poured down boiling pitch and lead but the Norse 'bound over themselves shields of wood' and made a hole in the soft stone of the wall with their axes. The Steward was killed by a Norse arrow, Rothesay fell and the Norse won much treasure and ransom of 300 silver merks. This vitally strategic castle was besieged again in 1263 when Haakon IV launched the final Norwegian assault upon western Scotland.

During the 13th century, Rothesay was strengthened by the addition of a gatehouse with portcullis, plus four projecting towers that allowed defending archers to enfilade or cover the ground in front of the walls. The Viking threat passed with the peace treaty signed at Perth in 1266 but Rothesay Castle was soon in foreign hands again. The English held it at various points during the Wars of Scottish Independence. It fell to Edward in the late 1290s but was taken back by the Scots following an assault from the sea led by Sir Robert Boyd of Cunningham in 1306. After the defeats of Dupplin Moor (1332) and Halidon Hill (1333) Rothesay was English again, held for Edward III, Plantagenet and self-styled Lord Superior of Scotland.

Further sieges ocurred in 1462, 1527 and in 1544 when the invasion of Scotland by the Earl of Hertford provided the pro-English faction amongst the Scottish nobility with opportunities for mischief. The Earl of Lennox captured Rothesay Castle in the name of Henry VIII but in reality his actions served only Lennox's own strategic interests. Like many other Scottish castles, Rothesay was damaged by Cromwell's troops in the 1650s and torched by the forces of the Covenanting rebel Argyll in 1685.

Aberdour has a good claim to be considered one of the oldest fortified residences in Scotland. The first castle was a wooden motte erected in the twelfth century by the de Mortimers. They were typical of the mercenary Anglo-Norman knights invited to Scotland by David I to stiffen his military capability. The first motte had been replaced by a high stone keep by 1240. The castle dominated a key stretch of the Firth of Forth and the waters beneath the tower are still known as 'Mortimer's Deep'. The remains of a Mortimer baron, famed for his wickedness, were being carried by boat for burial within the abbey on Inch Colm Island, till the Abbot called upon God for help. The bones of the impious baron ended up in the stormy Forth.

In the years after Bannockburn, Aberdour Castle and its rich estates were given by Robert the Bruce into the safe keeping of Thomas Randolph, Earl of Moray. Thomas was Bruce's closest friend and had played a key part in the war for Scottish Independence. Bruce gave thanks for his victory in 1314 sitting in the 'leper's squint' within the chapel of St Fillan that nestles next to the castle. By 1342 however, the castle had fallen into the grasp of the powerful Douglases, an ambitious noble house even by the rapacious standards of fourteenth century Europe.

Aberdour remained in the hands of the Douglases, Earls of Morton, until the family tripped up in the complex political intrigues of the sixteenth century. James Douglas held the highest offices of state under Queen Mary serving as her Lord High Chancellor and then as Regent of Scotland during her imprisonment in England. He was however implicated in the brutal murder of Mary's secretary Rizzio in 1566. Others suspected that he had a hand in the dramatic death of her second husband Lord Darnley, blown to smithereens at Kirk o' Field the following year. Her son James VI signalled his coming to power in 1581 by trying and beheading James Douglas for these unsolved crimes committed more than a decade before.

Aberdour and its lands were naturally forfeit to the Crown. Although the Douglases won their way back into James' favour, the long decline of Aberdour Castle had begun. The building was burned in 1688 and again during the 1715 Rising when dragoons were billeted there. This fine house was in turn, a barracks, a school room and a piggery before its rescue from ruin in the 1920s.

For most of the thirteenth century, Scotland enjoyed a period of relative stability. The kingdom was fortunate in having a run of three strong kings; William the Lion (1165-1214), Alexander II (1214-1249) and Alexander III (1249-1286); who defended their interests with vigour. There was little opposition to these successful monarchs from within the ranks of their own barons and the Courts of Scotland and England were generally at ease with each other. King and baron alike could get on with the serious, if expensive and time-consuming, job of strengthening their castles. It was in this period that many of the wooden Norman forts in Scotland were transformed into castles of stone.

The long years of prosperity also gave ambitious barons the chance to improve their social and political position. No family did this more effectively in the thirteenth century than the Comyns who owned several important castles before 1250 including Balvenie Castle near Dufftown in the lands between Strathspey and the Garioch. Soon after 1200, the Comyns married into the family of the Celtic Earls of Buchan and in doing so, not only gained lands throughout the north east of Scotland, but also positioned themselves closer to the throne. Other important Scottish families came to the fore such as the Stewarts, descendants of Walter the Hereditary Steward, who between 1150 and 1250 won lands along the lower Clyde for the Scottish Crown and for themselves. It was a Stewart knight who ordered a castle built at Brodick on Arran in the Firth of Clyde in the 1240s.

The possibilities that peace offered for getting on with unhindered castle construction can be seen at three great Scottish castles that date from this period. The de Vaux castle at Dirleton in East Lothian was a state-of-the-art fortification, consciously modelled on the latest continental ideas. Like the immense structure of Bothwell Castle, Dirleton was heavily influenced by the Chateau de Coucy in Picardy. With walls over sixty feet high and a massive circular donjon tower, Bothwell was built on a scale that had not been seen in Scotland before this time. Caerlaverock near Dumfries was not only impressive but made excellent use of the surrounding water features in the landscape. All three of these huge castles were thought to be impregnable, as was the equally giant structure at Kildrummy in Strathdon. These claims were put to the test in the last years of the century when Edward of England attempted to add Scotland to his Plantagenet 'Empire'. Caerlaverock and Dirleton were no match for Edward's war machines and surrendered after brief bombardments by mangonel. Bothwell Castle held out for a little more than three weeks although the resolute defenders of Kildrummy were only brought low by treachery and fire.

The Wars for Scottish Independence had serious implications for the owners of castles. Many noble families that were important at the start of the wars in 1295 were cast low in the course of them. The Comyns were ruthlessly eradicated by Robert the Bruce after 1308. Smaller families with a long Scotto-Norman ancestry such as the de Gourlays of Hailes Castle lost their fiefs and were replaced by new names in Scottish history such as the Hepburns of Bothwell. Patriot families were rewarded for their loyalty and in some cases, such as the Irvines of Drum Castle, still hold the lands and the castle that Bruce granted them after his crushing victory at Bannockburn. In the West, men that could be relied upon to support the Crown such as Archibald Campbell, first Captain of Dunstaffnage Castle, were put into key fortresses once the power of the Macdougalls was broken.

The West also saw a new style of stone castle building in the thirteenth century. These were the castles of enclosure such as Duart, Dunstaffnage and Skipness where local lords threw up a high, thick wall to protect their goods and followers. The buildings within their stone courtyards were usually lean-to structures at first but developed into powerful castles in time. This simple layout was also used in some southern castles, as at Loch Doon in Ayrshire, where the curtain wall hugged the coastline of the castle island in the middle of the loch.

For almost 700 years the name of Drum has been identified with the Irvines who held the castle through twenty four successive generations. Formerly a Comyn stronghold, Drum was gifted by a grateful Robert the Bruce to a loyal friend who had supported him throughout the war with England. William de Irwyn acted as Bruce's armour-bearer and personal guard through some of the darkest days of the war, and rode by Bruce's side at Bannockburn. Irwyn's reward was the Royal Forest of Oaks and the Tower at Drum that lay to the west of Aberdeen, granted by royal charter at Berwick in February 1323.

Drum was originally built in the 1280s to serve as a hunting lodge for Alexander III. The site lacked natural advantages and so the castle had to be exceptionally sound. Alexander invited Richard Cementarius, the first Provost of Aberdeen, to mastermind its construction. Cementarius raised a crenellated tower that was over seventy feet high and twelve feet thick. As an added precaution, the door was on the first floor and reached by a retractable wooden ramp. The castle well was hidden in a secret recess in the wall and later generations added a solid iron yett to strengthen the entrance. The continual feud between the Irvines and the powerful Keiths ensured that the watch at Drum remained vigilant.

Time and again, the Irvines demonstrated their loyalty to the Scottish Crown, fighting and dying at Harlaw in 1411, Flodden in 1513 and Pinkie in 1547. The Irvines even lent their Great Falcon, a giant bombard, to the Crown to help repel the English invasion under Protector Somerset. The 6th laird worked closely with James V in the 1520s helping him to extend the reach of royal justice and extirpate 'rebels, thieves, reivers, sorcerers and murderers' from the kingdom. Only the fifth master of Drum blotted the family copybook by killing and dismembering his chaplain Sir Edward Macdowall in the secret well chamber in a fit of rage. Arguing that he had caught the chaplain in 'flagrant delicto' with his wife, Irvine was pardoned but fined 100 merks.

The Irvine family's loyalty to the Scottish Crown brought trouble to Drum Castle in the turbulent religious struggles of the seventeenth century. Drum was besieged by Covenanters under General Munroe and realising that the castle's walls were no match for Munroe's artillery, his wife surrendered. Thereafter, Drum suffered the indignity of intermittent billeting by government troops, while the Marquis of Argyll besieged and ransacked the castle in 1644 and plundered it in 1645 laying waste the estates with thorough enthusiasm.

Loyal to the Stewarts, the Irvines came out in the 1715 and 1745 Risings. After Culloden, the 17th laird hid in a secret room in the castle but his Hanoverian pursuers spotted the freshly dug ground where the family silver had been buried. The Irvines of Drum survived and kept the castle, but their lands and wealth were largely gone.

A great pit by the walls of Balvenie records this site's first appearance in recorded history. It contains the bones of a Viking host destroyed by the Scots under Malcolm II in the Battle of Mortlach in 1005. The armies clashed along the banks of the Dullan Water and the hard-pressed Scots were in low spirits until Malcolm called upon St Moluag for divine assistance. Duly fortified, the Scots chased the Vikings northwards, slaughtering them on the brae where Balvenie Castle now stands. A grateful King Malcom extended the nearby Mortlach Church by the length of three spears and placed the severed heads of three Viking leaders in niches within the church as a warning to other Scandinavian invaders. One of these skulls is known to have provided sport for local schoolboys as late as 1760.

Despite this bloody start, the subsequent history of Balvenie Castle was relatively peaceful for it suffered no sieges during its long history. This is curious given its strategic importance. Sitting above the waters of the Fiddich, the castle controls the junction of roads between the rich lands of Aberdeenshire and Strathspey. As a stronghold of the Black Comyns, Balvenie was a key link in the chain of fortresses that linked their extensive landholdings in Buchan and Badenoch. The Lordship of Balvenie came into the hands of William Comyn, one of the new breed of Scotto-Norman aristocrats, when he married the last heiress to the old Celtic Earldom of Buchan in the early 13th century. His son Alexander probably built the first proper stone castle here, originally known as the Castle of Mortlach, on the site of an earlier Pictish fort.

In 1308 the Comyns were crushed by Robert the Bruce and after his 'harrying' of the Buchan lands, Balvenie Castle stood abandoned for some years. Local legend links the castle in the late fourteenth century to Alexander Stewart, the Wolf of Badenoch. Balvenie was certainly held by the family of the Black Douglas in the early 1400s but their ambition also aroused royal resentment. When James II wiped out Douglas power in 1455, Balvenie was given over to the safe hands of his kinsmen, the Stewart Earls of Atholl. They incorporated a fine Renaissance house within the magnificent thirteenth century curtain wall in time for the visit of Mary Queen of Scots in September 1562. In 1610 Balvenie passed from the Stewarts, and was bought by the Duff family who held it until the suicide of the last laird in 1718.

One of the strongest and most imposing castles in Scotland, Kildrummy Castle was built to control the roads between the rich provinces of Moray and Mar. Begun by the energetic Bishop Gilbert de Moravia around 1240, it was held for Alexander II and III by the Earls of Mar. Tradition holds that Edward I of England also contributed to Kildrummy's construction. Edward's favourite military architect, Master James of St George, was paid £100 while Edward was staying at the castle in 1303. Similarities between the gatehouses at Kildrummy and Harlech suggest that a Plantagenet hand was at work.

The work of Master James and his fellow masons was soon tested in the great siege of 1306. Defeated at the Battle of Methven, Robert the Bruce sent his wife Elizabeth and daughter Marjorie to Kildrummy for safety. Its defence was entrusted to his younger brother Sir Neil Bruce. After weeks of fruitless effort, the besiegers resorted to alternative methods. The castle blacksmith, Osborne, was bribed to start a fire and destroy the supplies of grain piled up in the castle hall. The heat of the fire was so great that the surrounding English troops had to retreat. When the castle garrison reluctantly surrendered, the treacherous Osborne received his payment. Edward ordered that molten gold be poured down his throat. Kildrummy suffered besiegement again in 1335 when Lady Christian Bruce held out against supporters of Edward III until relieved by the forces of her husband, the great patriot Sir Andrew Moray. When David II was captured at the Battle of Neville's Cross in 1346, Kildrummy was occupied by Thomas, Earl of Mar, who refused to hand it back to the King when he was ransomed in 1357. The castle returned to the Crown when David II successfully besieged it in 1361.

Subterfuge was used to win Kildrummy once more in the early fifteenth century when in 1404 assassins murdered the castellan Sir Malcolm Douglas. It was rumoured that they were in the pay of the ruthless Alexander Stewart, Wolf of Badenoch. Two years later, Stewart's plan became clear. He seized Sir Malcolm's widow Isobel, the Countess of Mar, and forced her to marry him. By this strategem, Alexander became Earl of Mar and holder of Kildrummy.

Kildrummy saw action again in the religious wars of the seventeenth century. Cromwell successfully ousted a royalist garrison in 1654, and it was manned by Jacobites under Viscount Dundee during the crisis of 1690. It was at Kildrummy that John Erskine Earl of Mar plotted the ill fated Rising of 1715 to restore the House of Stewart that ended on Sherrifmuir. With the Earl's exile in France, the castle's high quality ashlar stone was gradually removed to decorate houses throughout Strathdon.

In the long struggle for Scottish independence between 1296 and 1357, Bothwell Castle changed hands no less than five times as the outcome of the wars swung in the balance. One of the most impressive fortresses in the kingdom, it was circled by a wall that was sixty feet in height and fifteen feet broad. Its position on a bend in the Clyde valley six miles south east of Glasgow also meant that it controlled the routes in and out of western Scotland.

When Edward Longshanks invaded Scotland in 1296, Bothwell was one of his first targets. He quickly captured the castle, and its owner William Moray, brother of Andrew Moray who fell at Stirling Bridge in 1297. Thanks to a massive effort in a siege lasting fourteen months, the Scots won Bothwell Castle back during the winter of 1298-99 when the English garrison ran out of supplies. It was lost again in 1301 when Edward returned to Bothwell with a force of 6,800, many of whom were skilled military engineers. Edward also brought the Belfry, a high siege tower that was constructed in Glasgow and trundled to Bothwell on thirty hay wagons. The Belfry was designed to tackle the strongest point in Bothwell's defences, its massive circular donjon keep, modelled on the great Chateau de Coucy in Picardy. In case the Belfry failed, Edward also brought three giant ballistae and twenty three miners to undermine Bothwell's walls.

The Belfry did its job. The siege in August 1301 lasted little more than three weeks. Edward then made Bothwell Castle the centre of his administration in Scotland under Aymer de Valence, Earl of Pembroke. The English garrison there held out against the forces of the Bruce until 1314. After Bannockburn, the Earl of Hereford and the shattered remnants of Proud Edward's army fled to Bothwell for safety. The overwhelming manner in which the Bruce had crushed the English army however, made it impossible for Hereford to hold out and Bothwell Castle was surrendered to the Scots once more.

Bruce had the castle slighted and much of the keep was tumbled down into the Clyde. Enough remained for Edward III to use Bothwell as his base in his 1336 invasion. The following year Andrew Moray won back and destroyed his own ancestral home to ensure that it had no further military value. After 1362 the castle was rebuilt by Archibald the Grim but later members of his family used the stones of Bothwell for other Douglas residences.

Close to the English border, Caerlaverock Castle controlled the important waterways of the Solway and the Nith, the south western gateways to medieval Scotland. Built to a unique triangular shield design and surrounded by a moat, Caerlaverock was also protected by the rough Solway landscape of marshes, thickets and surging tides. Locals knew it as 'the island of Caerlaverock'. Its castellans were the fiercely belligerent Maxwells. No wonder that one chronicler in 1300 described it as 'so strong a castle that it feared no siege'.

Edward Longshanks respected Caerlaverock's reputation for impregnability. In 1300 the Plantagenet laid siege to Caerlaverock with a force of 87 knights and 3000 men, aiming to punish the Maxwells for their role in organizing resistance to him throughout the south west. Siege engines were brought from the castles of Carlisle, Lochmaben and Roxburgh. One of these was the Warwolf, a giant trebuchet that hurled 200 pound stone balls high over Caerlaverock's marshy defences. Ninety of these missiles smashed into the castle's towers and curtain walls before the terrified garrison of 60 Scots emerged to surrender.

Caerlaverock was now garrisoned by English troops although the castellan was still a Maxwell. However, when Sir Eustace Maxwell switched allegiance from Edward II to Robert I in 1312, an English army surrounded Caerlaverock once more. This time the Scots held out. After Bannockburn, King Robert offered various privileges to the Maxwell family as compensation for the demolition of the castle. Enough remained however for Sir Eustace to repair and pledge to the puppet king Edward Balliol in 1333. Caerlaverock was only recaptured by the Scottish Crown in 1356 when Roger Kirkpatrick took and demolished it.

Caerlaverock also suffered in later wars. The fifth Lord Maxwell was twice captured by the English, after the battle of Solway in 1542 and again in 1544. He was forced to surrender the castle into English hands as a guarantee of his future 'good' behaviour. The Earl of Sussex is said to have 'threwn down' the castle in the siege in 1570, though the damage from this siege was soon repaired. In the religious wars of the 1630s and 40s, the royalist Earl of Nithsdale held out in Caerlaverock against a besieging Covenanting force for thirteen weeks. Nithsdale's garrison of 200 starving men only marched out of the castle in 1640 when Charles I granted them permission to surrender with honour. The Covenanters proceeded to dismantle parts of the fortress which gradually fell into ruin.

Plague, rebellion, and witchcraft have all played a part in the history of Dirleton, in the rich county of East Lothian. An earlier 'place of strength' here was used by the Canmore kings before 1100. The barony was gifted to the Norman de Vaux family by William the Lion before 1200. They built a fortress on a craggy rock that dominated the lucrative pilgrim route road to the North Berwick ferry and the shrine of St Andrew in Fife. The de Vaux built their castle well. It withstood a long siege in 1298 until the Prince Bishop of Durham finally brought giant mangonels into play. Repaired by English troops, the Scots were unable to win back Dirleton in the next thirteen years. Although Bruce later slighted the castle, it remained one of the great bulwarks of the Scottish kingdom, and great families such as the Halyburtons and Douglases vied to control it.

In 1515 it came by marriage to the Ruthvens, a bold, ambitious family who lived on the dark edge of Renaissance politics. Patrick Ruthven was behind the murder of David Riccio at Holyrood. William Ruthven planned the coup of 1582, kidnapping James VI and holding him as his pawn. John and Alexander Ruthven were later killed in the mysterious Gowrie Conspiracy. The family lost Dirleton when they fell from power in 1600, their Earl dismembered in Edinburgh and their very name proscribed.

A short day's ride from Edinburgh, sixteenth century Dirleton boasted fine lodgings and splendid formal terraced gardens. It was a perfect retreat for the king when pestilence broke out in the wynds of old Edinburgh in 1585. The young James stayed in quarantine at Dirleton that May, feasting and play-acting until his host 'fell deidlie sicke'. The Devil himself turned up on the green beneath the castle wall in June 1649, taking the form of 'a greate blak man'. Several of his servants were held in Dirleton's pit prison, where the Devil's marks were found upon them by the witchfinder John Kincaid. They remained in the pit until the order for their execution by strangling and burning came through from Parliament.

The following year Royalist irregulars used Dirleton as a base for harrying Cromwell's lines of communication to Edinburgh. The success of these 'moss-troopers' stirred General Monck into action and in November 1650, 1600 roundheads and a battery of siege guns descended upon Dirleton. The royalist moss-troopers were quickly routed but 'the pleasantest dwelling in Scotland' was largely reduced to rubble.

Medieval warfare was often very brutal. That lesson was learned by the garrison at Hailes Castle in East Lothian in 1446 when the castle fell to the pro-English forces of Archibald Dunbar. Angered by the resistance of the Hailes garrison, Dunbar 'slew all of them that he found thairin'. Hailes was however well placed to resist most attacks. Sitting on an outcrop of rock, the river Tyne protected it to the north while its southern flank was defended by a deep moat and some of the earliest surviving stonework in Scotland. The postern staircase to the river could only be crossed by a drawbridge. Once the bridge had been retracted, this approach was defended by an insurmountable pit.

The first tower at Hailes was built in the 1290s by the de Gourlays, Northumbrian knights who owned estates in the Lothians until the Wars for Scottish Independence. The de Gourlays backed the losing side and forfeited their lands in Scotland as a result. Hailes was given by charter of David II to Adam Hepburn, a vassal of the Earl of Dunbar. In time, the ambitious Hepburns accrued the Earldom of Bothwell, turning their power base at Hailes into a strong redoubt. Close to the rich burgh of Haddington and the road from England to Edinburgh, Hailes was on the route of several invading armies. It was badly burned in 1532, and damaged again in the 'Rough Wooing' of 1544. In 1547 Patrick Hepburn opposed Regent Arran and was required to surrender the castle to the Scottish government. In February 1548 it fell to an English force under Lord Gray of Wilton. Regent Arran won it back however and removed its heavy iron gates to make sure that Hailes would be of little future use to English commanders.

Hailes was much enlarged and gentrified by James Hepburn, the fourth Earl of Bothwell. After abducting Mary Queen of Scots and forcing her to accompany him to his fortress at Dunbar, James became her third husband soon afterwards. Mary is said to have 'found his doings rude, yet...his words and answers gentle.' Fleeing from Borthwick Castle in May 1567, Mary and Bothwell spent the night of 5th May at Hailes en route to the capital. After the defeat at Carberry Hill, Bothwell fled to exile and death in Denmark. The Hepburns forfeited Hailes Castle which passed in succession to the Stewarts, Setons and Dalrymples. Like many other castles in southern Scotland, Cromwell's artillery brought Hailes castle's life as a effective fortress to an end in the 1650s. Its last owner, Arthur Balfour the former Prime Minister, bequeathed it to the nation in 1926.

Originally known as Balliol Castle, Loch Doon in Ayrshire was built after 1275 on a small island in the middle of the loch. Its unusual eleven sided outline stems from the fact that its curtain wall simply followed the shape of the islet. The depth of the surrounding waters made it difficult for besiegers to build a causeway out to the castle and it was far enough from land to be out of range of most siege mangonels and trebuchets. Besiegers could only hope to take Loch Doon by trickery, by negotiation with a famished garrison or by a hazardous ship-based assault. Nevertheless the castle was besieged several times.

The ancient seat of the Lords of Carrick, Loch Doon Castle first appears in documented history in the wake of Robert the Bruce's defeat at Methven in 1306. After helping the unhorsed Bruce back on to his steed, Sir Christopher Seton and the remnants of his men quit the field at Methven and made for the safety of Loch Doon. The castle governor, Gilbert de Carrick, believed that the House of Bruce was fully vanquished and handed Sir Christopher over to a besieging English force. Seton was promptly hanged at Dumfries.

Although today a much abused ruin, Loch Doon Castle has a very special place in Scottish history. In 1333, at one of the lowest points in the Wars for Scottish Independence, Loch Doon remained loyal to the Stewart cause and flew the standard of David II when almost every other stronghold in the land had declared for the English puppet Edward Balliol. Only five others, Dumbarton, Urquhart, Lochmaben, Lochleven and Kildrummy, remained true to the patriot cause. The example of Loch Doon's castellan John Thomson was the turning point that led to eventual Scottish victory.

The full power of the noble House of Douglas was unleashed against Loch Doon in 1446. William, the 8th Earl of Douglas, saw Loch Doon as an important strategic asset in his feud with the neighbouring Kennedy clan. Although Loch Doon Castle held out for several weeks, its small garrison was no match for the skill and resources of the Douglas military machine and the castle was surrendered.

By the late fifteenth century the castle was held by the ambitious Maclellans of Dumfries who tried to challenge the power of the Douglasses in Carrick. Loch Doon Castle was subsequently won back by the Kennedies when they in turn found themselves under attack in 1510, this time by Sir William Crawford of Lochmores. The Kennedies had gentrified the castle around 1500 by adding an oblong tower residence. They needn't have bothered, as the castle was burned down and seriously slighted in the 1520s by James V as part of his clampdown on the more unruly elements of the feudal nobility. The iron portcullis was cast down into the loch and has resisted several attempts since to raise it to the surface.

In the 1930s the level of the loch was altered by a hydro-electric scheme. The outer shell of the castle was dismantled in 1935 and faithfully re-assembled higher up the nearby shore, although much of the keep remains under the waters of Loch Doon.

Castle Tioram was the fortress of the Macdonalds of Clanranald who held the lands of Moidart and the isles of Rum, Canna and Eigg. It sits on a small tidal island and was an ideal location to watch the busy seaways between the southern Hebrides and Skye. Clan legend says that the castle was built by Amy MacRuary, the slighted wife of John, seventh Lord of the Isles. Archaeology however suggests that a simple fortress based on an enceinte wall has been on this site since the early 1200s.

On the orders of the Queen Regent Mary of Guise, the Earls of Huntly and Argyll attacked the Clanranalds in Toiram in 1544. Several canonballs from this siege were found embedded in the castle walls during repair works in 1888. Cromwell also occupied and garrisoned Tioram in the 1650s in an unsuccessful attempt to subdue the 'wild Papists' of the western Highlands.

Tioram was a castle of 'pit and gallows'. The clan chief had full legal and judicial powers over his land and his people, including the rights to imprison and execute. In the 1660s, the twelfth clan chief, John, was a sadistic man who enjoyed terrifying the local population. In his later years, he sat in the highest turret of Tioram with his favourite gun, nicknamed the Cuckoo, shooting at everything within range. This included several unfortunate clansmen coming to pay the rent to their mad laird. While John lived, Tioram was haunted by an unusual spectre. A large black frog is said to have followed the chief everywhere until the day of his death.

Tioram was destroyed in 1715 on the orders of its last occupant, Allan Mor of Clanranald. The chief was reluctantly setting out in support of the 1715 Rising and a seer had foretold his death at the impending Battle of Sheriffmuir. Allan Mor ordered his men to torch the castle declaring: 'I shall never come back. It is better that our old family house be given to the flames than forced to give shelter to those who are about to triumph over our ruin.' From a nearby hilltop, he watched his ancestral seat burn and crumble before heading east to fall at Sheriffmuir as prophesied.

Although now a deserted ruin, Tioram served the Jacobite cause once more in the '45 when French artillery for the Rising were hidden there. However the impoverished Clanranald lands could provide few horses to carry these heavy arms on the invasion southwards and twelve of Bonnie Prince Charlie's vital cannon had to be abandoned there.

Location matters in castle building. Duart Castle enjoys one of the finest defensive positions in Europe. Perched on the promontory of Dubh Ard or 'black point', Duart sits at the junction of three seaways; the Firth of Lorne, Loch Linnhe and the Sound of Mull. Control of Duart brought control of the sea trade between the Hebrides and Ulster. Duart was also the key link in a chain of castles along the Sound that allowed a message to be transmitted by beacon from Dunollie near Oban to far Mingary on Ardnamurchan.

Dubh Ard has probably been fortified since ancient times. A castle of curtain wall and courtyard was certainly there by the 13th century and it fell into the hands of Clan Maclean during the 14th. Lachlan Lubanach Maclean may have built the first stone keep after 1370. On the landward side, Duart's walls were over three metres thick. Perhaps this was needed to keep out Ewan Maclaine, the headless warrior whose ghost was said to ride along Glen Mhor to the south west of the castle.

Duart's fate however was always linked to the sea. In the 1520s, Lachlan Cattanach earned the enduring hatred of the Campbells when he chained his barren wife Margaret Campbell to a rock, hoping to drown her. Margaret was saved by a passing fisherman but her relatives took their revenge all the same, murdering Lachlan in his bed in 1527. The waters around the castle saved Duart in 1653 when a sudden storm sank two of Cromwell's besieging ships. Originally vassals of the Lords of the Isles, Chief Lachlan was kidnapped in 1608 after dinner with the King's Lord Lieutenant on board a royal ship in the Sound of Mull. The price of Lachlan's freedom was the destruction of his war galleys and an oath of fealty to James VI.

Thus began the Macleans' unwavering loyalty to the House of Stewart which was to cost them dear. After coming out for the royalist Montrose, Sir Lachlan Maclean could not hold Duart against the superior forces of General Leslie in 1647. In the 1650s the Macleans of Duart lost more men and money aiding the royalist cause, principally in the disastrous Battle of Inverkeithing in 1651. Their reward was heavy debt and to fall into the financial clutches of the Campbells. Duart was besieged in 1674 and again in 1688. While Sir John Maclean led his men at Killiecrankie, Campbell fleets bombarded Duart. The castle was finally lost after the defeat at Cairnburg Mhor in 1691. After the 1645 Rising, it briefly served as a garrison for Hanoverian troops who torched it when they left in 1751. The present day castle is the result of the impressive restoration masterminded by Sir Fitzroy Maclean between 1911 and 1936.

A fortress has stood on the broad rock of Dunstaffnage at the mouth of Loch Etive for over 1500 years. The early Scots of Dalriada had a stronghold here and this may have been the resting place of the sacred Stone of Destiny for several centuries after it was brought over from Ireland. The present castle was built by the Macdougalls, Lords of Lorn around 1225. The Macdougall masons had a keen eye for the landscape. Dunstaffnage, basically a quadrangular castle of enclosure in places over sixty feet high, is perfectly moulded to the great knob of conglomerate on which it sits. It is a tribute to the Macdougall castle builders that this Highland fastness remains almost entirely unaltered after more than seven centuries.

Macdougall politicians were much less skilled. The clan chose to support Edward Plantagenet against Robert the Bruce at precisely the wrong moment in the long wars of Scottish independence. Edward's death in 1307, and the rising wave of national belief in the Scottish cause, left the Macdougalls seriously exposed. Their opposition to the Bruce led to a crushing defeat at the nearby Pass of Brander in 1308. Once the royal army had penetrated into the lands of Lorn, the fall of Macdougall Dunstaffnage was inevitable. King Robert duly besieged and captured it in the following spring.

Dunstaffnage had already been the site of an earlier royal attempt to break the Macdougalls and their Norwegian allies, when Alexander II brought a 'great host' to Lorn in 1249. However with the royal fleet assembled in Oban bay, Alexander mysteriously fell ill and died on the neighbouring island of Kerrera. Another mysterious death in 1463 finally resolved the ownership of Dunstaffnage Castle. The murder of John, the second Stewart lord of Lorn, by a Macdougall assassin sparked six summers of bitter clan feuding in the area. The conflict only ended in 1470 with the Campbells of Argyll taking full Lordship of Dunstaffnage and Lorn, a key moment in their rise to influence.

The Captainship of Dunstaffnage Castle was first entrusted to a Campbell, Archibald, in 1322. With short periods of resurgent Macdougall and Stewart influence in the area, that hereditary post has remained in the hands of the Campbells of Dunstaffnage ever since. Although the castle is now in state care, the present Campbell Captain spends at least one night each year in the Gatehouse as a symbol of his clan's historic occupancy.

Sitting on flat grazing land near the empty shore lands of the Kintyre peninsula, Skipness Castle seems to be in an unusual location. The clue to its existence lies in the fact that its main entrance, once defended by a machiolated gatehouse tower and a portcullis, lies on the seaward side. Skipness was built as a base in the sea wars fought along the shores of western Britain between the Gaelic birlinn and the Norse longship. In the military geography of thirteenth century Scotland, Skipness was vital as it overlooked the confluence of four important waterways; the Firth of Clyde, the Sound of Bute, Loch Fyne and the Kilbrannan Sound between Kintyre and Arran.

Its strategic importance explains the sudden switch in the ownership of Skipness in the early 1260s. A charter of 1261 confirmed Skipness in the hands of Dugald MacSween whose family had spent the previous fourteen years heightening its great curtain wall. The following year however, as King Haakon's vast invasion fleet appeared in Hebridean waters, Skipness was entrusted instead to the Menteiths, kinsmen of the Stewarts. The King of Scots was making sure that Skipness was held, spoiling any secret deals between Clan MacSween and the Norse overlord.

At some point after 1400, Skipness became part of the Macdonald lordship of the western isles. Skipness was again a border fortress but this time it lay on the frontier between the Lordship of the Isles and the kingdom of the Scots. It was one of the Scottish Crown's first targets when James IV set out to crush the Macdonalds in 1493. At first it was held for the Stewarts by their Forrester allies but in 1499 it fell into the clutches of Clan Campbell. These were western magnates with whom the Stewarts could do business and Skipness Castle remained a Campbell house for almost four hundred years.

Campbell ownership was confirmed by charters of 1576 and 1588, and was only threatened once in an unsuccessful siege in 1644 by the Irish guerilla, Alastair Colkitto. A more serous threat to Campbell ownership of Skipness was the execution of the rebel Earl of Argyll in 1685. His opposition to the catholic James VII and II threatened two hundred years of careful acquisition of power by Clan Campbell. King James issued a warrant for 'the razing down of the strength at Skipness' but its canny captain, Walter Campbell, petitioned to save his home from destruction. James' reign proved to be brief and the subsequent monarch, William II & III, was friendlier to the Campbell cause. Skipness remained in their hands until 1867 when the impoverished Campbells of Skipness took the opportunity to sell it.

Brodick Castle has had many masters including an Irish King, Norse chieftains, and a French Duke. Its long and violent history is hard to imagine as the older fortifications are now masked by the stately home designed in 1844 by James Gillespie Graham in the Scots Baronial style. Brodick however has been described with some justification as 'Britain's most war-weary castle'. It was much fought over, largely as a result of its strategic location overlooking the Firth of Clyde and much of Scotland's south western coastline.

Broodick sits on a high wooded shelf at the foot of Goatfell, the ridged peak that dominates the Isle of Arran. Brodick means broad bay in Gaelic and is a reminder that the earliest known lords of the island were the Scotto-Irish kings of Dalriada in the Dark Ages. The site was later held by the Vikings, who drew their ships onto the beach below their fortress, until they were driven from Arran in the eleventh century. The first stone castle was raised by the Stewarts around 1240 but by 1260 it was in Macdonald hands. Edward Longshanks took Brodick at an early point in the Wars for Scottish Independence but it was re-captured by the Bruce in 1307. An English fleet sent by Henry IV badly damaged Brodick and briefly occupied it in 1406. Further damage was inflicted on the structure by the Macdonalds in 1455.

The Hamilton Earls of Arran took possession of Brodick Castle in 1503, prompting a flurry of military modernization in the next seven years. Nevertheless, it again suffered badly at English hands in 1544 during the 'Rough Wooing' of Henry VIII. Undaunted, the Earl of Arran, now rejoicing in his French title of Duke of Chateauherault, oversaw substantial repairs the following year. During the Wars of Religion, the Campbells and Hamiltons vied for control of Brodick, with it changing hands in 1639, 1644, 1646 and 1651. A Cromwellian garrison occupied it in the early 1650s, adding a new artillery battery to cover the approaches to the castle. It now houses the art collection of the eccentric author and architect William Beckford of Fonthill.

Brodick is a mysterious and much haunted place. Restoration work in 1977 exposed an abandoned staircase that led to a forgotten room, entirely contained within the thick walls of the keep. A solitary figure has been spotted sitting ruefully in the castle library, while the castle's Grey Lady is said to be the shade of a medieval unfortunate, thought to be carrying the Black Death and cast into the castle pit. A ghostly white deer grazes by the castle whenever the chief of the Hamilton family is near to death.

The High Middle Ages in Scotland were dominated by a struggle for control of the kingdom and the Crown. The royal House of Bruce, and then the House of Stewart, became locked in a conflict with a succession of great noble families who threatened to fatally weaken the kingdom of Scotland for their own dynastic ends. At times it looked as if the legitimate royal house would fail. Under weak kings such as Robert III or absent ones such as James I, powerful regents could usurp the royal powers for their own ends. The Stewarts fought back by playing the dynastic game better than anyone else, placing cadet branches into key roles. Thus relatives like the Stewarts of Darnley, later earls of Lennox, were made castellans of crucial Crookston Castle outside Glasgow. A very conscious effort was also made to encourage a sense of national loyalty to the Scottish Crown, and the Stewarts, with symbols such as the Thistle and the Lion Rampant adorning public places, castle walls and even the coins in every Scots purse. Eventually, the intelligent and resilient Stewart dynasty crushed the opposition.

The first of these rivals for power was the mighty Clan Macdougall who had dominated the western Highlands and the Hebridean islands in the thirteenth century, often siding with Norway against the King of Scots. Gaelic speaking princes of a sea-based culture, and masters of a string of stone castles along the Atlantic coast, they paid little attention to the distant king of lowland, farming Scotland. With the departure of the Norse after the Treaty of Perth in 1266, the Macdougalls looked southwards for potential allies. They naturally sided with Edward I of England against Robert the Bruce in the middle stages of the Wars for Scottish Independence. After Bannockburn in 1314, they paid the price. Macdougall lands and castles were confiscated and given to more reliable clans such as the Macraes at Eilean Donan Castle and the Campbells who eventually inherited the old Macdougall territories around the head of Loch Awe. Other proud and opportunist Highland chieftains such as the MacNeills of Kisimul Castle now had to time their raids upon the lowland kingdom with much greater care, waiting for the reign of a weaker monarch or the unsettled times that came with the minority of one of the Stewart infant kings. Ironically one loyal Highland clan that supported the Bruce was to pose an even greater threat to Scotland. The Macdonalds benefited enormously from the power vacuum in the western Highlands that followed the Macdougall collapse in 1320. By 1450, they had established a powerful, semi-independent principality through their Lordship of the Isles and sought alliances with the kings of England, planning to carve up the 'middle kingdom' of the Scots between the Sassenach and the Gael.

In the period 1300-1450 however, the greatest threat to the royal house came from the intricate family network of the Douglas Earls. By 1430 they could field an army every bit as powerful as any that a Stewart could command. They held the keys to some of the most powerful strongholds in Britain; none was more impressive and more impregnable than Tantallon Castle in its prime. In 1400 the most powerful man in Scotland was not the king but Archibald the Grim, the Douglas Earl who sat safely in his well protected island 'capital' of Threave in the south-west. To destroy such a dangerous rival, the Stewarts had to raise up many 'new men'. The McLellans of Kirkcudbright and the Cairns of Orchardton Tower were typical of the ambitious lesser gentry who served James II in his campaign against the House of Douglas, enjoying rich rewards in return. Both witnessed the siege of Threave Castle in 1455 and were soon building new fortifications of their own upon former Douglas lands. The Campbells benefited the most from loyal service to the Crown. Lesser folk in 1300, by 1450 Clan Campbell controlled much of Argyll and feared only the Macdonalds. Campbells also held great offices of state in the Stewart kingdom, a development which forced them to purchase Castle Gloom in the Ochil hills in order to be close to the Stewart Court at Stirling.

The island of Donan in Loch Duich has been fortified since the earliest recorded times. The remains of a vitrified fort and the impression of a human foot sculpted in stone are strong clues to activity here as far back as Iron Age times. The island and the castle take their name however from the seventh century missionary Donan who went calmly to his death on Eigg in 618 AD once his pagan executioners agreed to first let him finish Mass. The earliest records of a castle here date from the mid thirteenth century, at the time of the Norse withdrawal from western Scotland following their defeat at Largs in 1263. Alexander III is said to have given Eilean Donan to a warrior called Colin MacCoinneach, or Mackenzie, who had excelled in battle against the Norse. Ownership of the castle was then disputed between the Earl of Ross and Clan Mackenzie for some decades. According to tradition, the Mackenzies wisely befriended Robert the Bruce and sheltered him at Eilean Donan after his defeat at Dail Righ in 1306. The Mackenzie reward came in time from David II in the form of a charter confirming their ownership of the castle and its estates. However the clan most closely associated with Eilean Donan are the Macraes who acted as Constables there for the Mackenzies, earning the nickname 'Mackenzie's coat of mail'.

The Macrae's had a fearsome military reputation earned in bloody combats such as the Battle of the Park in 1488 where Big Duncan of the Battle Axe slew the champion of the Macdonald Lord of the Isles. After that the Macraes had to repulse several onslaughts upon Eilean Donan by Macdonald war-bands. Duncan Macrae finally settled the feud in 1539 when Eilean Donan was encircled by a Macdonald fleet of more than fifty warships. Macrae's arrow hit the great chief Donald Gorm Macdonald of Sleat in the foot, severing his artery and hastening his death at nearby Avernish.

More devastating weapons were available when Eilean Donan was briefly the centre of European affairs in 1719. The Spanish Crown agreed to try and restore the House of Stewart and a detachment of 300 Spaniards landed in Kintail to garrison Eilean Donan. In May three English frigates sailed into Loch Duich and pulverised the castle. Eilean Donan remained a ruin until the early 20th century when it underwent a remarkable transformation at the hands of John Macrae-Gilstrap who masterminded its renaissance as the most photogenic castle in Scotland.

Mingary Castle on the Ardnamurchan peninsula is the most westerly fortification on the mainland of Great Britain. Its Gaelic name, Mioghairidh, means 'the land between the machair and the moor', the point where the fertile sand dune pastures of Scotland's western coasts meet the darker peaty inland soils. The name is a reminder that when Mingary was built in the 1200s, these empty lands were populous and rich. The first castle was a high curtain wall that traced the roughly hexagonal outline of an outcrop of rock above the shore. The castle's main entrance faced the sea but on the landward side, the castle was open to attack from sloping ground to the north. The solution of the castle builders was to cut a 25 foot wide ditch out of the solid rock to protect that flank. Additional parapets and battlements were added in the sixteenth century to allow the use of muskets by the defenders. Difficult to approach or besiege, Mingary was a useful look out point from which to observe the sea traffic sailing towards the Sound of Mull and Loch Sunart.

The early history of Mingary Castle is obscure. The first stone castle was built 1265 by the Macdougalls but forfeited by them when they opposed the House of Bruce. David II granted the lands of Ardnamurchan to Clan MacIain who were confirmed in their ownership of Mingary Castle in 1499 after supporting James IV in his expedition against the Macdonald Lords of the Isles. A royal charter however was no protection against angry rivals. Mingary was besieged by the Macdonalds of Lochalsh in 1515 and captured by them two years later. The lands of MacIain were laid waste and Mingary was razed. The Chief of Clan MacIain was slaughtered in 1519 trying to win back the fortress. Although his heir Mariada sold her rights over Ardnamurchan to the Earl of Argyll in 1540, a MacIain was again living in Mingary in 1588. The arrival of the wind-tossed remnants of the Armada in the Hebrides that year provided opportunities for mischief. Maclean of Duart supplied food and water to the captain of the Spanish galleon Florida in return for his help against his foes in Mingary across the Sound. The attack failed but the rocky inlet beneath Mingary is still known as Port nan Spainteach, port of the Spaniard.

After 1612 the castle was held by the Campbells who repelled several attempts by neighbouring clans to prise them out. MacIain hopes of returning to Mingary were forever dashed in 1626 when the clan was hunted down as pirates by their erstwhile Campbell allies. Mingary suffered in the Wars of Religion, falling to Colkitto in 1644 and to General Leslie three years later. Charles Edward Stewart's arrival in nearby Moidart in 1745 terrified the local Campbell parish minister and a garrison of Hanoverian redcoats was dispatched to Mingary with all possible speed. As the area was cleared of people in the following years, Mingary became an isolated, though striking ruin.

Although a small and simple domestic fortress, Clackmannam Tower is rich in royal associations. Its links with the Kings of Scotland begin with its origins as a hunting lodge in the late thirteenth century and end with the ceremonial award of a mock knighthood to Robert Burns there in the 1780s. Consisting of two high towers built of pink and golden sandstone, Clackmannan Tower was closely linked to the House of Bruce and it remained in their hands from the early fourteenth until its abandonment in the late eighteenth century.

A short ride from Stirling Castle only six miles to the west, Clackmannan Tower sits on top of the King's Seat Hill, giving views along the Firth of Forth, across the Ochils, and northwards to the hunting forest of Tillicoultry. The Tower also helped to defend the small medieval port of Clackmannan that grew up at the point where the Black Devon river met the shifting, silting waters of the upper Forth. Raiding by Highland clansmen was not impossible here and so the Tower was equipped with a large iron brazier for signaling to other strong points in the vicinity. Local tradition claims that the lodge at Clackmannan was much used by Robert the Bruce but the earliest surviving record of the Tower is a grant by his son David II to a bastard kinsman called Robert Bruce in 1359. Nevertheless Bruce is linked to the Tower by the ancient but spurious tale of how he left his mannan or gauntlet upon a clach or boulder. He ordered his squire to 'look aboot ye', a command remembered in a local place name and in the motto of the 'wee county', Clackmannshire.

The last Bruce owner of Clackmannan was Lady Catherine Bruce who lived on in the Tower after the death of her fiercely Jacobite husband in 1772. Lady Catherine took great pride in her royal lineage and owned a number of medieval artifacts including the helmet and sword of Robert I. She used his great unwieldy weapon to knight favoured visitors to the Tower including Robert Burns who knelt before her to be dubbed in 1787. The castle was abandoned on her death in 1791. Like many other derelict Scottish castles, the agricultural improvements of the nineteenth century exacted a heavy toll on Clackmannan Tower. The sixteen century mansion house next to it was soon recycled into local farm buildings and the 1815 parish kirk. Mining subsidence inflicted further damage on the Tower in 1955, now much repaired in recent years by Historic Scotland.

Named after a holy man that lived by the nearby Liddel Water, and close to the border between Scotland and England, Hermitage Castle was no place for quiet contemplation in the Middle Ages. Described as 'the guardhouse of the bloodiest valley in Britain', this grim fortress has a dark history. According to legend, the first castellan, Nicholas de Soulis, dabbled in witchcraft and child abduction but thought himself indestructible thanks to a prophecy that he could never be harmed by steel or bound by rope. The local people duly wrapped the baron in bands of lead and boiled him in a brass cauldron at the nearby stone circle of Nine Stane Rig. The building of the first castle by de Soulis in 1242 almost sparked an English invasion of Liddesdale when Henry II objected that this massive fortress was too close to the Border.

In the fourteenth century, a later Custodian of Hermitage, William Douglas, imprisoned a rival for the post of local Sheriff in Hermitage's dungeons until the unfortunate Sir Alexander Ramsay had starved to death. The de Soulis family lost Hermitage in 1320 as a result of a plot to assassinate Robert the Bruce. In both Wars for Scottish Independence, Hermitage fell under English control but in 1338 Sir William Douglas the Knight of Liddesdale besieged it. Sir William had survived the disastrous defeat at Halidon Hill in 1333 and two years in English captivity. After the surrender of Hermitage, he held it as his own until he was murdered by his godson in 1353. The oldest parts of Hermitage date from the time of Sir William and his English successor Hugh D'Acre. The third Earl of Douglas added the great corner towers in the 1390s. In the fifteenth century the Douglas Earls of Angus were instructed by a suspicious James IV to exchange Hermitage Castle for estates nearer Glasgow. In this way Hermitage came into the hands of the Hepburns.

In October 1566, Hermitage was held by James Hepburn, 4th Earl of Bothwell. Badly wounded in a skirmish with some southern rievers, Bothwell was carried to his bed within the castle. Hearing of this, Mary Queen of Scots set off from Jedburgh at once, riding wildly to be at Hepburn's side. Mary covered fifty miles of tough moorland that day and the chill that she caught after a tumble in the marshes almost killed her. When the last Bothwell Earl died in Naples in poverty and disgrace in 1624, the castle and its estates passed to the Scotts of Buccleuch. With inadequate artillery defences, Hermitage was rendered obsolete in the seventeenth century and abandoned.

The ruins of Strathaven Castle in South Lanarkshire sit on a prominent rocky mound above the well preserved conservation village that shares its name, near the Powmillan Burn that flows towards the Water of Avon a short distance away. The first castle at Strathaven was erected by a branch of the Baird family, descendants of le seignur de Bard who fought at Hastings with Duke William of Normandy, and of the Henry de Barde that attended the court of William the Lion in the 1170s. The adjacent name of Flemington is an additional clue to Strathaven's origins as a typical feudal settlement from the period of Normanisation in southern and central Scotland.

The first stone castle of Strathaven was built around 1350 but was burned down in the 1450s. By then the castle and its surrounded estates had passed from the Bairds to the Sinclairs and then to the Black Earls of Douglas. Its destruction in the mid fifteenth century was probably the result of Crown action, part of the successful efforts of James II to curb the power of his more unruly magnates. Strathaven seems to have been deliberately slighted around 1455, the same point in time that the House of Black Douglas was defeated and disgraced at Threave Castle near Dumfries. After several years in the hands of the Crown, James II gifted the castle to his loyal kinsman Sir Andrew Stewart, Lord Avondale, who began much of the structure that survives today as well as providing its alternative name. In 1534 Strathaven was acquired by the Bastard of Arran, Sir James Hamilton of Finnart, a talented military architect who served James V as Master of the King's Works. Finnart may be responsible for some of the sixteenth century finishing touches at Strathaven, such as the wide mouthed gun loops that can still be observed on the ruin.

Strathaven is a mere seven miles south from the burgh of Hamilton. As the power of the Hamilton family increased, it was inevitable that Strathaven would fall within their sphere of influence. It passed to the Marquesses and Dukes of Hamilton in 1611 and remained in their hands for the following three centuries.

A local tradition tells that the wife of a Strathaven laird so displeased her husband that he resolved to entomb her alive within the castle walls. She was led to a niche, blessed by a priest and walled up forever. Part of the walls collapsed in a storm in the middle of the century, revealing a collection of human bones.

O n the grassy hill of Dundonald, the tower or hillfort of Donald has been a fortification for millenia. Recent excavation has revealed evidence of human activity on the site before 2000 BC while a Dark Age fortress was vitrified by an exceptionally fierce fire before 1000 AD. The reason for Dundonald's importance is clear when one climbs to the site of the present castle. The hill of Dundonald not only dominates the surrounding countryside near Troon in South Ayrshire but offers distant views as far as Ben Ledi and Ben Lomond over 40 miles away to the north. Seawards, it looks out across the Firth of Clyde to Arran and beyond to Kintyre and the Paps of Jura.

Throughout historic times, Dundonald has been indissolubly linked with the Scotto-Norman House of Stewart. Walter the Steward raised a motte and bailey castle of earthworks and timber on the hill soon after arriving in Scotland in 1136. Alexander, the Fourth Steward of Scotland, replaced this primitive structure with an impressive stone castle around 1260, perhaps in anticipation of the Norwegian invasion of western Scotland two years later. Alexander's fortress was one of the largest castles in medieval Scotland but it was completely destroyed in the Wars for Scottish Independence in the early fourteenth century. The present castle was built by Robert II in the early 1370s, perhaps to mark his accession to the throne. Robert certainly loved Dundonald, spending much of his time hunting on its estates and dying there in 1390. Dundonald served the Stewarts well once more when James I returned from imprisonment in England to find his authority challenged by his most powerful noble subjects. James cannily went back to the loyal Stewart homelands around Dundonald Castle when his reign was threatened in 1425. With his kinsman John 'the Red Stewart', he raised his standard at Dundonald and amassed an army there for the victorious campaign against the rebel Earl of Lennox and Murdoch, Duke of Albany.

The later Stewart monarchs were less enamoured by the gaunt, grey tower of Dundonald. It was now too distant from the new Stewart power centres of Stirling, Falkland and Edinburgh. James III finally sold it off to the Cathcart family in 1482. In the 1630s and 1640s later owners, the Wallaces and Cochranes, used Dundonald as a quarry for their more fashionable and comfortable residence at nearby Auchans Castle. The Lower Hall at Dundonald still features a very fine example of a medieval barrel-vaulted ceiling while the western wall displays five stone heraldic shields which are amongst the oldest in the country.

Thanks to Shakespeare, the names of Cawdor and Macbeth are inextricably linked. Cawdor was already a thanedom or earldom in the eleventh century and Macbeth may have known the original fort at Old Cawdor, a mile north of the present site. His successor Malcolm Canmore granted Hugh de Kaledouer lands and titles for his help in restoring Malcolm's family to the throne. A strong, loyal hand was needed as Cawdor, only six miles east of Inverness, lay close to the wild Highlands. The Crown strengthened old Cawdor Castle in 1398, yet several Thanes met violent deaths policing this frontier.

The present fortress dates from the fourteenth century. In 1454 James II granted the Thane permission to crenellate his tower, on condition that the King could enter and depart without hindrance. Tradition says that the Thane followed a dream when selecting a location for his tower. A donkey laden with a kist of gold was let to roam the countryside until it came to rest beneath a tree. The castle was built around the tree which still stands in the castle dungeons after more than five hundred years. Unfortunately the donkey was no military architect and Cawdor's site offers few defensive advantages. To compensate for this, the castle was surrounded with a moat and given walls so thick that they housed a secret pit prison. The great yett or iron gate was carried in triumph to Cawdor after the Thane destroyed Lochindorb Castle in Strathspey in 1455.

Like many Highland fortresses, Cawdor fell into Campbell hands. In 1499 the Earl of Argyll was given powers of wardship over the infant heiress Muriel. As the Campbell troops came to collect the child and carry her to the West, her mother burned her with a red hot key and bit off the tip of her finger so she could be identified at a later date. Despite these forebodings, Muriel's later marriage to Sir John Campbell was a happy and fruitful one. A local legend claims that the Campbells will hold Cawdor for as long as a red headed maiden lives by the shores of Loch Awe.

In the 18th century, a later Thane made the mistake of declaring his Jacobite sympathies. After 1745 the family chose to live quietly on its Welsh estates, far from Cawdor and Culloden. Fortunately this self imposed exile ensured that Cawdor was spared later 'improvements' and it remains a perfect mixture of late medieval fortress and Jacobean home. It is also believed to house three ghosts; a lady in blue, the shade of Sir John and a Campbell maiden whose father amputated her hands in an attempt to impose some distance between the girl and her unsuitable lover.

The history of Crookston Castle on the southern edge of Glasgow is one of chivalry and romance, a fact obscured by its current besiegement by the housing estate of Pollock. The first castellan Robert de Croc was an archetypical Norman knight and a vassal of Walter, the Hereditary Steward of Scotland. Robert was exactly the kind of knightly landowner who helped to spread the feudal system throughout central and eastern Scotland in the twelfth century. Around the year 1190, he built a wooden motte and bailey castle surrounded by a dry moat and a thorn-hedge, on a hogback ridge three miles south of Paisley. The village that grew up around the motte provided the corrupted name of 'Crookstoun'. The castle was a well chosen look out spot with long views over the Clyde valley and the fertile fields of Renfrewshire.

In the 14th century, the castle and its lands passed to the Stewarts of Darnley whose most illustrious member, Sir John Stewart, distinguished himself in the Franco-Scottish massacre of the English at Baugè in 1421. As Count of Evreux in Normandy, Sir John became Constable of the Scots in France in 1428. Although he died in the Siege of Orleans, a goodly portion of the ransoms that he won in France were sent home to help complete the transformation of Crookston Castle from a tower of wood into one of stone. The mason's work at Crookston faced its most serious test in 1489 when the holder, now Earl of Lennox, rebelled against the young King James IV and a price of a thousand merks was put on his head. James took this first test of his authority seriously and a powerful siege train that included the giant Flemish bombard Mons Meg was sent to pulverize Crookston. The castle held out for little more than a day and the king and Lennox were soon reconciled.

Crookston was besieged again in 1544 when Regent Arran sought to weaken the troublesome Lennoxes. The garrison again surrendered before the siege artillery did much damage to the castle's fabric. The Darnleys forfeited Crookston Castle in 1544 but had regained it by 1565 when it was the home of Henry Darnley. Mary Queen of Scots and Darnley are said to have been betrothed under the ancient yew tree at Crookston and they certainly spent some time there after their marriage in July 1565 at Holyrood. After Darnley's assassination, it passed to minor and illegitimate lines of the Stewart clan and was wholly ruined by the 18th century. It has the honour of being the very first property acquired by the National Trust for Scotland, having been gifted to the Trust in 1931 by one of its founder members Sir John Stirling Maxwell.

In the years after 1500 Clan Campbell held much of western Scotland in a tight grip. Kilchurn Castle was a key link in the chain of strongholds that sustained Campbell power. Sitting at the head of Loch Awe, Kilchurn blocked access from the east through the narrow Pass of Brander and to the lands of Lorn beyond. Although today the castle sits on a thin peninsula, in the 15th and 16th centuries it sat on a small island linked to the shore by a secret causeway hidden below the surface of the water. Originally a five storey tower house, Kilchurn was also protected by a curtain wall that enclosed most of its island base, and by three corner towers added in the late 17th century.

The tower house at Kilchurn was begun around 1440 when the captain of Kilchurn was Sir Colin Campbell of Glenorchy whose crusading exploits earned him the nickname of the Black Knight of Rhodes. According to tradition, his wife Margaret busied herself overseeing much of the construction of the tower during his absence overseas. The MacGregors of Glenstrae acted as keepers of Kilchurn until falling out with the Campbells in a violent feud in the early seventeenth century. The castle was besieged by Royalists under General Middleton for two days in 1654 until relieved by Cromwellian forces sent in haste by Monck. It was besieged again in the troubled year of 1685 when the Protestant Earl of Argyll rebelled against the Catholic James VII. Kilchurn was garrisoned with Hanoverian redcoats as soon as news of the 1715 and 1745 Risings reached the ears of the government in Edinburgh. Sir John Campbell, who became 1st Earl of Breadalbane in 1681, was aware that Kilchurn's strategic position in the turbulent western Highlands was worth good money. Around 1690 he built a barracks block at Kilchurn capable of holding over 200 troops and then tried to sell the castle to the government as a ready-made fortress. His plans were only thwarted by the government's decision to expand its base at Fort William at the head of Loch Linnhe, which was more easily supplied by sea.

In the eighteenth century, the Campbells of Breadalbane paid more attention to their more fertile estates in Perthshire and they moved in 1740 to Balloch Castle, later known as Taymouth Castle near Kenmore. Kilchurn was abandoned and badly damaged by lightning in 1769. The sad loss of its roof the following year encouraged local builders to use Kilchurn as a convenient quarry. In 1817 drainage work on the outflow from Loch Awe lowered the waters and attached the castle more securely to the surrounding land.

The history of Kisimul is linked to Clan MacNeill, a typical Hebridean family with Norse, Irish and Celtic blood in their veins. The MacNeills began to build the sea fortress of Chiosmuil (the rock in the bay) off the south coast of Barra in the Western Isles in the 1040s. Once established in their sea fortress, the MacNeills went on to play a leading part in the history of Highland Scotland in the Middle Ages. MacNeills led the men of Barra to victory at the battles of Largs in 1263 and Bannockburn in 1314. Independent and much respected, the pride of Clan MacNeill was summed up by the story that during the Biblical Flood, the chief refused Noah's offer of hospitality in the Ark on the grounds that 'the MacNeill had a boat of his own'. Each evening, the chief's Piper would ascend the battlements of Kisimul to signal that 'the great MacNeill of Barra having finished his meal, the other princes of the earth may dine.'

MacNeill had reason to be proud. Kisimul was an impregnable fortress, a three story tower within a curtain wall that almost completely enclosed the rock on which the castle stands. Two artesian wells and a fish trap ensured that the castle could withstand the longest siege. The clan birlinns or galleys were berthed beneath the castle crewhouse, ready to be launched in minutes. Kisimul easily withstood several assaults in the sixteenth and seventeenth centuries by rival clans. In lean times, MacNeill chiefs could resort to piracy with impunity, knowing that they were very distant from the courts of the King of Scots. The MacNeills could only be subdued by trickery. One was invited to treat with James V at Portree on Skye in 1540 and promptly imprisoned despite the King's promise of safe conduct. The 15th Chief, Ruari the Turbulent, was ordered to explain his capture of an English ship, an act which displeased Elizabeth I and embarrassed James VI. The MacNeill ignored the royal summons but fell to a familiar Highland stratagem. He was invited to come down from the ramparts of Kisimul and feast aboard the galley of Mackenzie of Kintail. Mackenzie plied his guest with whisky until MacNeill was reduced to helplessness, carrying the chief to Edinburgh where he was tried for piracy. MacNeill saved himself however, arguing that his actions had been prompted by a desire to revenge the King's mother Mary, executed by the English Queen.

MacNeill was spared but had to acknowledge Mackenzie's superiority for his estates and Kisimul. The castle was abandoned in the nineteenth century but the ruined structure was marvellously restored in the 1930s by the American architect Robert Lister MacNeill. In 2000 Kisimul was leased to Historic Scotland for a thousand years for an annual rent of one pound and bottle of whisky.

Circular towers have been built in Scotland for millennia as brochs such as Mousa and Glenelg prove. Medieval masons also knew that rounded towers deflected missiles better than angular ones. It is surprising then to note that Orchardton Tower overlooking the Rough Firth on the Dumfries-shire coast is the only circular tower house in Scotland. There are however similar towers in Ireland and Orchardton is a reminder of the strong trading links between south west Scotland and nearby Ireland. Over thirty feet high, Orchardton enjoys commanding views of the locality. The walls, tapered like a broch and machiolated for the dropping of missiles, are nine feet thick while the parapet is reached by one of the narrowest spiral staircases in Scotland. The Tower and its adjoining courtyard buildings were once protected by a generous barmkin wall, since quarried by local builders.

Built in the late 1450s on the site of an earlier Douglas stronghold, its first owner, John Cairns, was given the surrounding lands of Irisbuitle by James II for his part in overthrowing the house of Douglas. Cairns probably assisted at the royal siege of Threave castle in 1455. The Cairns held Orchardton uneventfully until 1600, although one scion, William Cairns, was involved in the fracas in 1527 that led to the murder of McLellan of Bomby by Gordon of Lochinvar at the door of St Giles Cathedral in Edinburgh. The succession to Orchardton was disputed in the late sixteenth century when the family ran out of male heirs and the property was divided between several daughters and their husbands. It took the wealth of Sir Robert Maxwell to reunite the estate in 1615 and Orchardton remained in Maxwell hands until the bankrupt 7th Baronet Orchardton sold the tower and the land to the Douglasses in 1785.

Sir Walter Scott visited Orchardton and heard the tale of its most famous owner, Sir Robert Maxwell. As a boy Robert was cheated out of his rightful inheritance by conniving relatives and sent away to France. Enlisting at 15 in a French regiment, he distinguished himself at the battles of Dettingen and Fontenoy in the 1740s. After sailing to Scotland in November 1745, Robert was wounded at Culloden. His status as a French officer saved him from the butchering meted out to most of the defeated Jacobites left on the moor. Some years later while back in France, he learned of his claim to the Orchardton estate and pursued it in the Scottish courts, finally becoming Baron Orchardton in 1771 when the House of Lords decided in his favour. Robert's tale subsequently inspired the plot of Scott's Guy Mannering.

Doune Castle is an impressive place of strength. Protected to the west by the River Teith, and by the Ardoch Burn on the east, it sits on a high promontory on the very edge of the Highland line. On this well chosen site, its masons raised a fearsome stronghold. The thick rectangular gatehouse is over 95 feet high and was even higher when built in the late 14th century. The castle gateway leads past a portcullis and iron yett into a long, murderous, vaulted passageway, punctuated with arrow loops, that lasts for more than forty deadly feet. Not surprisingly, Doune Castle was a very secure fortress and seldom changed hands as a result of military action.

In prehistoric times, an earthwork fortification or dun stood on the site although little remains except the corrupted placename of Doune. Most of the present castle was built by Robert Stewart, the first Duke of Albany who was king of Scotland in all but name during the reign of the feckless Robert III and the minority and exile of James I. Albany died in 1420 and the castle was briefly held by his son Murdoch until his execution by James in 1424. Doune became a royal fortress and being only eight miles from Stirling, it was used as a hunting lodge by the Stewart Court. It also served as a dower house for three widowed Stewart queens; Mary of Gueldres, Margaret of Denmark and Margaret Tudor. The castle also held out loyally for another Stewart Queen, Mary Queen of Scots, until 1570, two years after her flight to England. In the late 16th century, the Stewart captains of the castle gained the titles of Lord Doune and Earl of Moray. Doune has belonged to the Earls of Moray since 1590.

Sitting astride one of the main roads from Highland Scotland, Doune was inevitably a busy place in the years of religious tension. It was occupied by the Marquis of Montrose in 1645 and by garrisons of government redcoats during the Jacobite risings of 1689 and 1715. It was taken by the forces of Prince Charles Edward Stewart in 1745 and entrusted to the governorship of MacGregor of Glengyle. After the Jacobite victory at Falkirk in January 1746, Doune Castle housed their many prisoners who included the young Rev. John Witherspoon, later the architect of the American Declaration of Independence and an energetic President of Princeton College. Roofless in the later eighteenth century, Doune became a ruin but enjoyed a sympathetic restoration by the Earl of Moray in 1883. A well preserved and authentic medieval castle, it featured in the movie 'Monty Python and the Holy Grail'.

Crichton Castle in Midlothian was home to one of the great Machiavellian figures of Renaissance Scotland. Son of a minor baron, Sir William Crichton used his position as a courtier to acquire power and wealth, rising by 1439 to the great offices of state as Master of the King's Household and Chancellor of Scotland. Sir William was unafraid to employ the darker arts of statecraft, planning the Black Dinner of 1440 at which the young Douglas lords were assassinated in the presence of the king. The unsuspecting boys were even welcomed into Crichton Castle where they dined and rested en route to their deaths in the capital. Crichton's murderous behaviour was remembered by the young king who stripped Crichton of his offices when he assumed power in 1444. The castle was then besieged and stormed by royal forces under Sir John Forrester of Corstorphine in 1445.

The Crichtons had acquired their estates only a generation before when Sir John de Crichton received a charter of barony from Robert III. The castle that stands on a bend in the river Tyne near the village of Pathhead was probably begun by Sir John around 1375. All was lost by the third generation when the 3rd Lord Crichton was stripped of his lands by James III in 1484 after fathering an illegitimate child with the king's sister Margaret and siding with the rebel Duke of Albany. Under James IV, the confiscated Crichton lands were granted to Sir Patrick Hepburn, the Earl of Bothwell. The adventurous 4th Earl of Bothwell, James Hepburn, burst on the scene in 1559 when he sallied out from Crichton Castle to intercept an English mission which was carrying 4,000 crowns from Elizabeth to aid the Protestants in Scotland. In retaliation, the Protestant Lords under the Earl of Arran besieged and captured Crichton. Bothwell had regained it by 1567 however when he 'abducted' and married Mary Queen of Scots.

Bothwell's subsequent exile and death in a Danish prison left Crichton without a laird. It was given in 1581 by James VI to the wild and desperate Francis Stewart by virtue of his Hepburn mother. This educated ruffian had spent time in Italy and was responsible for Crichton's masterpiece, the diamond faceted courtyard facade modelled on the Palazzo dei Diamanti in Ferrara. Close to Edinburgh, Crichton Castle was convenient for ambitious courtiers such as the Crichtons and Hepburns. When the Court moved to London in 1603 the Castle lacked any strategic value and it slowly fell into ruin.

Set on a rocky promontory above cliffs overlooking the Firth of Forth, Tantallon was arguably the greatest fortress of Renaissance Scotland. Its main strength lay in its fifty foot high and thirteen foot thick curtain wall that separated the castle from the rest of Scotland. In front of the wall a deep ditch was cut into the rock and protected by flanking towers. The projecting central tower was converted into a barbican in the fifteenth century and a triangular ravelin or gun platform was added in the foreground in the early seventeenth century. Tantallon also had one of the deepest wells in Scotland as well as its own seagate. It was not only a strong castle but it had an impressive battery of artillery, second only to the forces of the king. It was little wonder that the English ambassador who resided at Tantallon in 1543 wrote to Henry VIII assuring his master that; 'Temptallon is of such strength as I need not feare the malice of myne enymeys.'

Tantallon was begun after 1350 and became the seat of the faction of the Red Douglas Earls of Angus. Powerful magnates, the Earls of Angus treated with the kings of Scotland and England on almost equal terms. In 1491 the 5th Earl, Archibald Douglas, plotted with Henry VII to depose James IV. The Stewart responded by launching a ferocious attack on the castle, supervising the siege himself from his flagship The Flower which was anchored by the Bass Rock close by, blockading the castle from the sea. An artillery train brought the heavy ordnance from Edinburgh Castle, subjecting Tantallon to a lengthy investment. Further Douglas treachery led to a second royal siege in 1528 when the 6th Earl held the young King James V under arrest for more than two years. Escaping in 1528, James besieged Tantallon for twenty days with an army of more than 20,000 men but he only succeeded in taking the castle the following spring by using the traditional Stewart skills of bribery and wily negotiation. Rebuilt as a royal fortress, Tantallon was modernized by 1543 and its central barbican largely rebuilt in rounded, softer stones that were more capable of withstanding cannonshot.

A force of Covenanters stormed Tantallon in 1639 hoping to free their co-religionists imprisoned on the Bass Rock. After Cromwell's invasion in 1650, Tantallon served as a base for a detachment of Royalist moss-troopers or irregulars. Monck was sent to extirpate this nuisance and with 2000 men and 16 heavy guns, he left his mark upon Tantallon, reducing it in a twelve day bombardment to the ruin that survives today.

Sitting high on a spur of the Ochil Hills, between the Water of Care and the Burn of Grief, Castle Gloom offers a daunting prospect. Fortified since prehistoric times, the site above a chasm (glom in Gaelic) controls the old drove road between Fife and the North and offers commanding views of the Forth valley. Originally a Stewart fortress, Castle Gloom was acquired by Colin Campbell, the first Earl of Argyll, in 1481. Campbell's power base was in the west, but he realised the need for an eastern foothold nearer to the movers and shakers at the Stewart Court. Gloom was secure yet only ten miles from the royal palace at Stirling; ideal for entertaining influential friends and clients while its deep pit dungeon could hold the politically inconvenient. Colin Campbell changed the name of the castle by Act of the Scottish Parliament in 1481 and succeeding earls enlarged the original keep into a residence worthy of one of the great families of State.

Castle Campbell played its greatest part in Scotland's history in 1556 when the Protestant firebrand John Knox preached the new Reformed faith there to the fourth earl and his retinue. Winning the powerful Campbell clan to the cause ensured the complete success of the Protestant revolution four years later in 1560. The so-called John Knox's Pulpit in the castle garden commemorates this decisive moment. It was however Campbell involvement in the religious intrigues of the early modern age that led to the castle's demise.

In 1645 the royalist Montrose gave detachments of Maclean and Ogilvy troops the opportunity to damage their covenanting Campbell enemies. Castle Campbell held out, though the surrounding 'lands of Dolour and Gloome' were laid waste. Argyll had his revenge in 1651 when the turning wheel of fortune saw him witness the execution of Montrose, hung drawn and quartered in Edinburgh's Grassmarket. Argyll had initially supported Charles II, placing the Scottish crown on the young king's head at Scone in 1651. However the crushing success of Cromwell's roundheads at the Battle of Dunbar later the same year forced a swift rethink in Campbell allegiances. Argyll declared for the Lord Protector. For this temporary disloyalty, the Campbell earl himself went to the block in 1661 but by then Castle Campbell had suffered occupation and burning by Cromwell's troops in 1653-54. The Campbells quickly won back royal favour but later earls chose to dwell in a residence within the burgh of Stirling. The ruined Castle Campbell fell upon truly gloomy times.

In the mid 16th century, St Andrews Castle was the bloody scene of one of the longest and most bitter sieges in Scotland's history. As new Protestant ideas from Europe spread through the land, leading Catholic churchmen tried to burn out the infection of heresy. In March 1546 the Lutheran reformer George Wishart was burned at the stake in front of the castle in the presence of its principal resident, the Archbishop of St Andrews, Cardinal David Beaton. In retaliation, a band of Protestant lairds from Fife entered the castle three months later disguised as workmen. Taking its garrison by surprise, they murdered the Archbishop and stabbed him to death, hanging his naked body from a window in the castle tower. Protestant diehards, including John Knox, flocked to St Andrews to hold the fortress against the government of Regent Arran. The siege that followed was long and bloody. The besiegers attempted to tunnel and mine under the castle but were foiled by defensive countermining. The siege only ended when a French fleet arrived off the coast of St Andrews to bombard the Protestant survivors into submission and pack them off to the galleys of the French fleet.

The siege of 1546-47 was not the castle's first taste of military action. Churchmen in medieval Scotland had always played an active part in the military affairs of the kingdom. It was after all Bishop Lamberton of St Andrews who led the decisive charge of the 'sma folk' at Bannockburn. The bishop's residence had to be a well defended one. The site of the castle on the rocky north shore of the burgh was fortified as early as the 1100s and had become the Bishop's main residence before 1200. Protected by steep cliffs and rock-cut ditches on the landward side, the site was well chosen. Nevertheless St Andrews fell to English siege twice in the Wars for Scottish Independence, in 1304 and 1330. It was only permanently recaptured in 1337 after which it was seriously slighted lest it be used by English forces again. After Flodden, the castle was brought into the age of artillery; two massive circular blockhouses or gun towers were built by Archbishop James Beaton and the castle was equipped with a battery of modern cannon. After the Reformation in 1560 the castle was used as a prison for political prisoners. It was well suited for this role, having a 24 foot deep bottle dungeon into which victims could be dropped and forgotten. In time the ruined castle passed into the hands of the burgh council who used its crumbling stones to repair and extend the harbour pier.

The coming of Cannon 1450-1550

Throughout the Middle Ages, local powers in every part of Europe could defy the wishes of the central authority - as long as their walls were high enough and their donjons well enough stocked with food and water. That all changed in the fifteenth century with the coming of effective siege artillery. Monarchs with well-organised governments were able to convert their taxes into military power on an unprecedented scale. The citadels of semi-independent lords and cities across the continent were soon tumbling. Thus the French kings could absorb the old principality of Brittany in the 1530s. Ancient self-governing cities in Italy such as Siena capitulated to the King of Spain almost simultaneously. Not for nothing did the French kings inscribe the barrels of their cannon with the words ultima ratio regis - the last argument of the King.

The same processes that tilted the balance of power away from nobles and other lordships towards the Crown were at work in late medieval Scotland. The Douglas Earls in particular had been a thorn in Stewart flesh since the 1370s but they were safe from royal retribution while siege cannon were unreliable and ineffective. After 1440 however, the Scottish Crown got its hands upon better, stronger guns. James II was the first Stewart king to benefit from the new technology and he quickly became an artillery enthusiast. His pet project of Ravenscraig Castle in Fife was built to withstand an artillery siege and to use the counter-attacking power of guns against any assailants. The array of guns at Blackness Castle near Linlithgow gave the Crown the power to seal off the Firth of Forth from enemy shipping. By the 1450s James had built up an impressive artillery train and a squad of experienced gunners, many from Flanders and France. The Crown was now strong enough to go to war against its deadliest rivals.

The royal campaign against the House of Black Douglas in 1454-55 was the first artillery war in Scotland. A string of Douglas strongholds quickly fell to the Crown; these were older, obsolete castles with no defences against cannon. Finally in the summer of 1455 the King and his men arrived at the Douglas 'capital' of Threave to pit their wits against a fortress that had been prepared for the most modern kind of war. The old medieval tower at Threave was now the core of a complex of artillery defences. Three circular gun towers provided offensive capability. Older outbuildings had been demolished so the gunners in the Earl's 'artillery hoose' had a clear line of sight. In the latest Italian style, the walls at Threave had been thickened and battered, or sloped, to lessen the impact of incoming missiles. It was too strong for King James' men and Threave easily withstood a two month siege. The castle eventually fell to the traditional combination of starvation and intrigue.

With the Douglases reduced and their lands distributed to more reliable, grateful 'lesser gentry', the Stewarts could concentrate upon humbling their Macdonald rivals in the West. Here again, new technology gave the King an edge. Western warlords had always felt safe from the king due to their sheer distance from the centres of royal power in the Central Lowlands. Advances in shipbuilding and artillery wiped out that geographical security. In the 1490s, Newark Castle on the Clyde became the base for Stewart operations against the Macdonald Lordship of the Isles. The combination of stronger guns aboard larger ships spelled the end for the semi-independent principality of the Gaelic world. The clan chiefs lined up to honour the king and his artillery as his fleet proceeded along the Atlantic shores.

Despite being on the far north western edge of Europe, new ideas from the Continent quickly made their way to Scotland. One example of this was the deadly caponier or secret gun tunnel that Hamilton built at Craignethan Castle in the 1530s. Another was the speed with which the Reformation transformed Scottish life. By 1550, the kingdom was split by new, ideological divisions. The resulting conflicts were to have significant consequences for the castles of Scotland. The utter destruction of St Andrews Castle by a French bombardment in 1547 pointed the way to the future.

The lairds of Borthwick Castle, twelve miles from Edinburgh, offered their prisoners a chance to win their freedom. With their hands tied behind their back, the prisoners could jump from one of Borthwick's towers to the other, twelve feet away. Those who succeeded were given their liberty. Those who failed were freed from earthly cares, for with towers rising to over 110 feet, Borthwick is the tallest tower house in Scotland.

Built in 1430 to a U plan with fourteen feet thick walls, the twin towers of Borthwick were defended by a curtain wall, several circular towers, a thickened gatehouse and shot-holes. The eastern side was protected by a ditch, and the entrance to Borthwick was by drawbridge and portcullis only. The north tower was eight storeys high and afforded comfortable living. The heraldic chronicler Alexander Nisbet was impressed by Borthwick's great hall; 'It is so large and high that a man on horseback could turn a spear in it with all the ease imaginable.' Mary Queen of Scots dined and danced in Borthwick's Hall in 1563 and again in June 1567 after her marriage to Bothwell at Holyrood. The arrival of a force of over a thousand men led by the angry nobility of Scotland left Mary in little doubt that her choice of partner was unpopular. Bothwell slipped away while Mary negotiated with the nobles who planned to murder the Earl. Once he was safe, Mary herself escaped by disguising herself as a page boy and climbing down from one of Borhwick's windows to a waiting horse below.

During the seventeenth century Wars of Religion, the Borthwicks remained loyal to the Stewarts. After Cromwell's victory at Dunbar in 1650, the castle was invested by a Parliamentary force. In fact Cromwell offered the royalist John, 10th Lord Borthwick, an honourable surrender promising him the opportunity to 'carry off your arms and goods and such other necessitate as you have'...'if you necessitate me to bend my cannon against you, you may expect what I doubt you will not be pleased with'. Borthwick was surrendered after a brief demonstration by Cromwell's artillery men who fired off a devastating salvo against the castle's eastern wall.

Borthwick has two ghosts; one a serving wench who bore a Borthwick bastard in the Red Room where she was slain, the other a lawyer who acted as chancellor for the Borthwick family estates and who was burned to death after his creative accounting was exposed. Ruined in the eighteenth and restored in the late nineteenth century, Borthwick Castle was used as a secret repository for national treasures during the Second World War and is now a hotel.

Caisteal Stalcaire, the fortress of the Hunter, sits on the Rock of the Cormorants, an islet at the mouth of Loch Laich. The first castle on this site was built by the Macdougall Lords of Lorn but the present castle was raised by the Stewart Lords of Appin in 1388. Much of the surviving castle was built by Sir John Stewart before his murder at Dunstaffnage in 1463 by a renegade Macdougall. Five years later the castle witnessed the revenge of his clansmen when they crushed their Macdougall foes in the Battle of Stalc fought at the castle gates.

A cousin to the Stewarts of Appin, James IV enjoyed hawking in the western Highlands. James stayed at Castle Stalker on several of his hunting expeditions, a fact commemorated by the improvements made to the castle's living quarters during his reign, as well as the royal arms above the front door. After James' death at Flodden in 1513, the influence of the Appin Stewarts waned and they found themselves at loggerheads with the rising House of Campbell. That rivalry was symbolized by the Campbell assassination of Sir Alexander Stewart while fishing in Loch Laich in 1520 and the murderous revenge taken by his son Duncan of the Hammers a generation later by killing nine Campbells in 1544.

In 1620 the castle fell into the grasp of Clan Campbell. Local tradition says that the 7th Stewart laird drunkenly wagered the castle in exchange for an eight oared wherry. More likely, the impecunious Stewarts of Appin succumbed to the lure of Campbell cash and sold it. In the civil war of 1688-90, the Stewarts briefly seized Stalker back, acting in the name of King James VII. After the victory of the Protestant Cameronians at Dunkeld however, Stalker was besieged by Campbell forces and the Stewarts quit the castle honorably in 1690.

In 1745, three hundred Appin clansmen besieged Stalker but could make little headway against a Campbell garrison of sixty. The shot from the Jacobites' two pounder cannon merely bounced off Stalker's thick walls. This failure to take Castle Stalker was to prove costly for the Jacobite cause, as it promptly became an important stop on the supply route between Inverary and Fort William as the Hanoverian government prepared to crush the Rising. After Culloden, the Western Highlands were ruthlessly 'pacified' and Stalker served as a mustering point where clansmen were required to surrender their weaponry. Abandoned and ruined by 1840, Stalker was sympathetically restored in the 1960s.

Craigmillar Castle in Edinburgh has a dark past, linked to plague, murder and at least one horrible death. Less than three miles from Edinburgh yet perched high on a hill in a rural setting, Craigmillar's air was considered very healthy in the late Middle Ages. Several monarchs used the castle as a convenient retreat when pestilence was raging through the narrow wynds of the city. James III also used Craigmillar in 1477 to imprison his brother John, Earl of Mar, who later died mysteriously within the castle's walls. The discovery of a skeleton walled into the castle vaults during restoration work in 1813 added to Craigmillar's notorious reputation.

In 1566, Mary Queen of Scots ordered a refurbishment of Craigmillar after the murder of her secretary Rizzio at Holyrood Palace. Craigmillar Castle was much more secure than Holyrood and was just far enough away from the plotting and intrigue that spilled out of the taverns along the High Street and Canongate to calm Mary's nerves. She remained there during the winter of 1566-67, refusing to follow the advice of her half-brother Regent Moray that she should divorce her husband Lord Darnley. Mary's refusal sealed Darnley's fate however, for several of her nobles then met at Craigmillar to plan the murder of the Queen's Consort. Darnley was 'blawn up wi gunpooder' at Kirk o'Fields the following March. The neighbourhood below the castle is still called 'Little France', a memory of the winter in which the castle village was crammed with French courtiers and servants waiting upon the Queen.

Craigmillar was an important link in the chain of fortifications that defended Edinburgh from invasion. Overlooking Arthur's Seat and one of the main routes into the capital, Craigmillar was within sight of Edinburgh Castle which allowed for the passing of messages by flashing mirrors and beacon braziers. The castle that is currently on the site was begun by Sir Simon Preston in 1374, probably replacing a wooden fort held by John de Capella. A particularly fine machiolated curtain wall and circular angle towers were added after 1427. The bailey, which held supply buildings, a chapel and gardens, survives today in excellent condition, despite being burned badly by the Earl of Hertford in 1544 during the 'Rough Wooing'. The gun loops in the castle doocot or dovecot are a reminder that the residents of Craigmillar had to remain vigilant even in the course of their daily domestic routines. The Prestons eventually sold the castle to John Gilmour in 1660 but it was ruined by 1800.

Fergus, the Celtic Earl of Galloway, had built the first fortress at Threave around 1100 but that was destroyed by Edward Bruce in 1308 when the Gallovidians sided with Edward Longshanks.

The Bruce kings needed a strong arm in the south west and David II chose the Black Douglas family to hold the Western March. Archibald the Grim became Lord of Galloway in 1369 and made Threave his power base shortly afterwards. Ruling his estates with as much power as any king he built the brutal stone tower which survives today. The castle sits on an island in the river Dee two miles west of the town of Castle Douglas, and was surrounded by a fortified village that could only be approached by boat. It had the added advantage of being far from Edinburgh allowing the Earls of Douglas scope to rule unhindered. A winch lifted military supplies to the higher floors during a siege while an exaggerated corbel under the battlements offered a place from which to hang enemies of the Douglas. McLellan of Kirkcudbright dangled here in the mid 15th century when he fatally crossed Earl William.

Threave was upgraded in 1447 to meet the threat of artillery. The buildings surrounding the castle were demolished to provide a clear line of fire for the castle gunners, and their stones cannibalised to build a low outer 'gun-werk' or artillery wall. Circular towers and a moat added to Threave's defences but James II was outraged when he learned that Henry VI of England had provided the cash for these improvements. James was spurred into action against the Douglas house, murdering the Earl at Stirling in 1452 and besieging Threave three years later. The king supervised the siege in person, inspecting the royal ordnance which included the great Flemish bombard Mons Meg. Despite these efforts, Threave held out for several months and only surrendered once James offered lands to the castle officers.

After 1526 Threave was held for the Crown by the Maxwells as hereditary custodians, apart from a brief English occupation in 1544 and several moments of crisis in 1565, 1568 and 1588 when the Maxwell castellan was suspected of treason. Threave was besieged by Covenanters for thirteen weeks in 1640 before its royalist garrison accepted the offer of an honorable surrender. The roof was promptly removed and the castle abandoned. It did serve as a cold and leaky prison for French prisoners in the Napoleonic Wars and now offers visitors an atmospheric visit.

Called Kilmarnock Castle until 1700, Dean Castle was home to the Boyds, followers of the Hereditary Steward in his campaigns to win territory in the west for the Kingdom of the Scots. Robert Boyd took part in the victory over the Norse at Largs in 1263 and was rewarded with estates in Ayrshire. During the Wars for Scottish Independence, Robert's son was murdered in the massacre of Scottish lords and knights carried out at Ayr in 1296 on the orders of Edward of England. The grandson of the line, Sir Robert Boyd, dedicated himself to revenge, serving with Wallace at the subsequent Burning of the Barns in Ayr and acting as the Guardian's second-in-command. When Wallace was executed in 1305, Sir Robert put his sword at the disposal of the Bruce, riding with him through the difficult years after the defeat at Methven in 1306. In recognition of his military skill, Boyd was given command of the right wing of the Scots army at Bannockburn in 1314. Boyd's division successfully withstood the charge of the English cavalry that day and in reward, he received the lands of Kilmarnock and West Kilbride in 1316.

Much of the surviving construction at Dean Castle dates from the mid fifteenth century when the Boyds were raised to the peerage by James II in 1454. Known for his honesty, Lord Boyd was made Regent of Scotland for the infant James III in 1460. The family's new social status was acknowledged in the architecture at Dean; the comfortable apartments known as the Place or palace were raised between 1455 and 1468. Unfortunately, Regent Boyd had little opportunity to enjoy his palace as the jealously of other noble houses led to his downfall and flight into exile in 1469. Surviving this setback however, the Boyds recovered their lands at Dean and were granted royal permission to found the nearby burgh of Kilmarnock in 1592.

Later Boyds were loyal adherents to the Stewart cause. Charles II expressed his gratitude for this by making William Boyd the 1st Earl of Kilmarnock. Later members of the family suffered for their loyalty to the Scottish royal family. The 4th Earl served with Prince Charles Edward Stewart in 1745 and was captured after Culloden in 1746. His lands and titles forfeit, the Earl was taken to London and beheaded alongside Lord Balmerino. This fulfilled a horrific vision at Dean Castle some years earlier when the Earl's servants saw his severed head rolling around the castle floor. Damaged by fire, the castle passed through several owners including Lord Glencairn, the friend of Robert Burns. It now houses a fine collection of arms and musical instruments.

Drummond Castle near Muthil in Strathearn has been home to two Queens of Scotland, a Hapsburg Knight of the Golden Fleece and a Governor of Smolensk in Muscovy with an interest in torture. The castle was begun around 1490 but the family had been servants of the Crown for several centuries by that point. Clan legend suggests descent from a Hungarian prince who accompanied St Margaret to Scotland in 1068 but the Gaelic name of Druiman, meaning a ridge of high ground, suggests more humble origins in the hill country to the west.

Sir Malcolm Drummond is credited with the destruction of the English cavalry at Bannockburn. He realized that the Scots' schiltrons, formations of poorly armed spearmen, were no match for the superior English horse. He ordered his men to strew caltrops, sharp four-pointed iron stars, on the ground ahead. These brought down the English horses and allowed Drummond's men to deal with the helpless English knights, trapped in their armour and the mud. The Drummond's reward was the right to carry the caltrop on his coat of arms, as well as lands in Perthshire.

The Drummonds remained close to the Scottish throne thanks to the beauty of their womenfolk. Margaret Drummond married David II in 1363 and the beautiful Annabella married the future Robert III three years later. James IV planned to marry another Margaret Drummond but jealous nobles hastened her early death with poison. Not everyone fancied the Drummonds however and their feud with the MacGregors lasted for a century. When John Drummond cropped the ears of some MacGregor poachers, they revenged themselves by beheading him and demanding bread and cheese from the victim's sisters. When the women provided some food, the MacGregors produced Drummond's head from a bag and crammed the victuals into its mouth.

In 1605 James VI elevated the clan chief to the Earldom of Perth but by 1650 it was Cromwell's men who were enjoying the castle and its fine gardens laid out in 1630. Like many disappointed Royalists, Sir William Drummond went into exile and ended up as a trusted servant to the Russian Tsar. While in Muscovy, he noted the efficiency of the thumbscrew and introduced these instruments to British torture chambers. In 1689 Clan Drummond remained loyal to the Stewarts, tasting victory briefly at Killiecrankie and elevation to the Jacobite Dukedom of Perth. The Drummonds came out for the Stewarts at Sheriffmuir in 1715, and again in 1745 when the Duke commanded the Jacobite left flank at Culloden. Even the Duchess of Perth was imprisoned for sheltering the fleeing Prince Charlie at Drummond Castle and for destroying the tower so it could not be used by the Hanoverians. The clan lands were forfeited until 1784 and their titles only restored in 1830.

For almost a thousand years the East Lothian fortress of Dunbar has been at the centre of events in Scottish history. The impregnable castle site in Dunbar harbour was defended by the Votadini tribe in Roman times, held by Northumbrian and Pictish warriors in Scotland's 'dark ages' and was finally captured by Kenneth MacAlpin, King of Scots in 849 AD. In 1072 Malcolm Canmore granted the lands and title of Earl of Dunbar to a Norman knight Cospatrick, whose son had raised the first stone castle here by 1140. The English King John failed to take Dunbar castle in 1214 but eighty years later Edward Longshanks was more persuasive. The 9th Earl of Dunbar swore fealty to King John Balliol and then to Edward I, helping the English to besiege Caerlaverock in 1300 and holding Dunbar Castle against the Bruce until 1314. When Edward II fled the field of Bannockburn, he made for his ally at Dunbar in search of shelter and a fast ship south.

In 1338 Lady Agnes, Countess of Dunbar, proved to be a patriotic chatelaine, as befitted a woman with Bruce blood in her veins. In her husband's absence, she held the castle for five months, prophesying that 'the Thistle would out-thorn the Rose' and this proved to be the case, thanks to Sir Alexander Ramsay and his men who braved the rocky coastline to bring in supplies from the sea. Agnes well understood the power of psychological warfare, sending bread and wine to her famished besiegers and ordering her maids to parade in their best linen along the castle battlements to wipe away the marks made by English missiles.

Half way along the coastline between Berwick and Edinburgh, Dunbar was of immense strategic value in the Border wars of the later 1300s and 1400s. The key to Scotland's south-eastern flank, Dunbar changed hands several times as a result of siege and treaty. The Scots Parliament finally ordered it to be slighted in 1488 to make it less attractive to invading English commanders. James IV rebuilt the castle in 1494 in time for it to be attacked by the Earl of Hertford in 1544 and be badly burned by German mercenaries under the Earl of Shrewsbury in 1548. A royal castle after 1435, an English spy in 1537 noted that James V frequently rode in secret at night to Dunbar Castle to check the expensive batteries of artillery that he had gathered there. His daughter Mary appreciated Dunbar's security, fleeing there in March 1566 two days after the murder of her secretary Rizzio. Little more than a year later, Mary was forcibly carried off to Dunbar by her abductor the Earl of Bothwell, accompanied by eight hundred pikemen.

The strength and importance of Dunbar so worried the Scottish Parliament that it was dismantled in the 1570s. The demolition of this once mighty fortress was completed in the 1840s by the Victorian inventor Robert William Thomson who demonstrated his new technique of detonating explosives by electrical charge on the ruins of Dunbar.

Newark's great moment in history came in the 1490s when James IV decided to move against the Lordship of the Isles. By 1400 the Macdonald Lordship was an almost independent princedom of sea, loch and mountain that ranged across the Hebrides and the Western Highlands. Lord Macdonald could call upon an army of mercenaries and a fleet of birlinns or war-galleys. His court at the palace of Finlaggan on Islay was a rich centre of Gaelic culture where bards and scholars gathered. Although a vassal of the King of Scots, Lord Macdonald entered into a secret treaty with Edward IV of England in 1462, agreeing to a joint attack upon the Scottish kingdom which was to be dismembered by the two princes. On learning about these plans in 1475, James III confiscated some Macdonald lands and extracted a promise of good behaviour from the Gaelic lord. However further restlessness in the Macdonald lands with the Battle of Bloody Bay on Mull in 1481 and a rebellion by the warlord Angus Og in 1493, convinced James IV that he had to impose tighter royal control. James had inherited a full war-chest from his avaricious father and had the advantage of being the first King of Scots since Robert the Bruce to speak Gaelic and to know the Highlands and Islands. He called on his lords to meet him at Newark Castle on the Clyde. The shipyards nearby and the store rooms within Newark Castle were to be busy places over the following months. James made several expeditions to the west between 1493 and 1495 until the Macdonald Lordship was crushed. Newark served as a useful base for these crusades, being close to Glasgow yet only a short sea journey away from the Gaeltachd, the Celtic world of the west.

In medieval times, Newark Castle at Port Glasgow controlled the point on the Clyde where ships had to berth on account of shallow water. The castle consisted of a tower begun in the early 1400s by the Maxwells of Calderwood and a splendid mansion house added in the 1590s by Sir Patrick Maxwell, a murderer of great charm and learning. After killing the laird of Skelmorlie and his eldest son, Maxwell calmed the furious younger son who had come for his revenge by reminding the angry youth that he, Maxwell, had made him 'laird o' Skelmorlie in ae day'.

Newark Castle was bypassed and decommissioned in the 1600s when a deep channel was dredged along the Clyde and ships could sail closer to Glasgow. The castle declined into a rope manufactory and a storeroom for a dealer in big cats and bears.

In the mid fifteenth century, a new breed of improved cannon exploded against castle walls throughout Europe and changed the course of history. Renaissance monarchs realized that improvements in artillery technology now gave them the power to subdue independent towns and haughty barons. James II was a typical Renaissance prince and shared the enthusiasm of his European colleagues for the power of artillery. James realized that science had at last provided him with the means to bring the unruly nobles of Scotland to heel. He also realized that to be safe on the throne, he had to build and hold a new style of castle that could withstand a possible rebel bombardment. Ravenscraig Castle near the site of Kirkcaldy in Fife was part of James' plan to build a series of new fortresses that could both withstand and return artillery fire.

The fortress at Ravenscraig was begun in the spring of 1460 on a site that was close to the rich trading burgh of Dysart and overlooked the broad bay of Kirkcaldy where fleets could moor and shelter before setting out across the North Sea. James' plan was to build two immense horseshoe towers of ashlar, fourteen feet thick and steeply raked at the base, capable of withstanding the force from the most modern guns of the age. When finished, the towers at Ravenscraig measured 43 and 38 feet in diameter. Both were furnished with narrow gun-ports to accommodate light short range cannon such as falconets. Each tower even had its own well so that it could survive independently in a long siege. A cross range between the towers provided a broad gun platform from which the defenders could harass any besiegers. Below this platform, a deep ditch cut through the headland rock separated the castle courtyard from the rest of the mainland. Steep cliffs on the seaward side added to Ravenscraig's impregnability.

James II never saw his completed fortress of Ravenscraig. In the summer of 1460, he tried to take advantage of the civil war in England between the Yorkists and Lancastrians by recapturing the long lost castle of Roxburgh on the border with England. James was killed in the course of the siege at Roxburgh, a victim of his deep curiosity for all things connected with artillery. One of his own siege bombards overheated and exploded, and the king was killed by flying splinters of wood and metal shrapnel. His widow, Mary of Gueldres, continued to oversee the construction work at Ravenscraig until her own death in 1463. Ravenscraig then lay unfinished for some years until James III persuaded William Sinclair, Earl of Orkney, to exchange Kirkwall Castle for the incomplete fortress in Fife. The Sinclair family finished the works and used Ravenscraig as a home until the Cromwellian invasion of Scotland in 1650. Like many other strongholds along the coasts of Scotland, Ravenscraig was garrisoned by Roundhead troops in 1651. It gradually fell into ruin but was used by the Royal Navy as a store in the First World War.

Craignethan in South Lanarkshire is one of the great artillery fortresses of Renaissance Europe. Its builder, Sir James Hamilton of Finnart, had travelled in France and Italy studying developments in military architecture. As Master of the King's Works, Sir James was responsible for construction work at royal sites such as Stirling and Falkland. However he produced his masterpiece between 1532 and 1540 when designing his own fortress of Craignethan Castle, the last great private castle of serious defensive capability to be built in Scotland.

Six miles north west of Lanark, Craignethan sits on a high rocky bluff that falls away steeply on three sides to the confluence of the River Nethan and Craignethan Burn below. A massive rampart and a deep dry ditch protected the western flank. The ditch concealed Craignethan's deadly secret which was covered over by rubble after the demolition of the rampart in the 1580s and then lay forgotten until 1964. At the bottom of the ditch, Finnart had constructed a caponier or covered tunnel from which his gunners could inflict withering fire on attackers. Its survival at Craignethan proves that Sir James was aware of the innovative work of the great Renaissance military architect, the Sienese engineer and artist Francesco di Giorgio Martini, inventor of the 'capannata' or little hut. Unfortunately the narrowness of the ditch at Craignethan restricted the gunners' field of fire, and the clouds of acrid gunpowder smoke given off by sixteenth century hand arms must have suffocated the troops posted in this ill ventilated corridor. The caponier was soon obsolete and its function given to a transverse wall at the end of the ditch.

Sir James Hamilton was implicated in a treason plot in 1540 and James V used this opportunity to execute his architect and confiscate his property. Soon back in Hamilton hands however, Craignethan was captured in 1568 after the Battle of Langside by the Earl of Moray, the Regent for the infant James VI. A siege was avoided when the Hamilton garrison decided to surrender without resistance. The Hamiltons had recaptured Craignethan through trickery by 1570 when they assassinated Regent Moray as he rode through the High Street of Linlithgow. The insane 3rd Earl of Arran lived at Craignethan in the 1570s but the castle's outer defences were largely demolished when the Hamilton family was indicted for their political crimes by James VI in 1579. After a brief life of fifty years, Craignethan Castle was abandoned and fell into ruin. It may have inspired Tillietudlem Castle in Sir Walter Scott's novel Old Mortality.

Before the Union of 1707, Dundee was one of the wealthiest ports in Britain and Dundee's taxes were crucial to the Scottish exchequer. James II recognised the need to defend the sea approaches to Dundee along the wide estuary of the river Tay. In 1454 he granted a licence to the Earl of Angus to build a fort at Broughty, several miles to the east of Dundee. By the time the five storey tower was completed in the 1490s, it was in the hands of Lord Gray of Foulis. He was given licence to hold Broughty Castle by James IV in 1490 as well as enjoy the lucrative fishing rights along the nearby coastline.

Others soon recognised Broughty's importance to the security and prosperity of the Scottish realm. In 1547 Lord Gray was approached by English ambassadors who were aware of his opposition to the Catholic princess Mary Stewart. In September Gray agreed to open Broughty to an English force. The English troops immediately set about strengthening Broughty's artillery defences, ravaging much of the rich Angus countryside in search of building supplies as well as food. The head of the Scottish government, Regent Arran, ordered a blockade of Broughty Castle but the English were able to sally forth at will, capturing and fortifying the strategically important Hill of Balgillo. Arran responded cautiously by building up in Dundee a well-equipped force of over 3000 French, German and Scottish troops that included 100 pikemen, 100 horse and 100 hagbutters or gunmen. In February 1550 this international force under the French captain des Thermes moved on Broughty's outlying defences with such vigour that the English garrison promptly surrendered.

Broughty Castle was handed back into the safe keeping of the Gray family, who were its castellans until the Cromwellian period. General Monck marched on the castle in August 1651 in order to oust the royalist Grays. In the face of superior numbers and resources, the Grays left the castle without a fight. It was restored to them at the Restoration but sold to the Fotheringhams in 1666.

Robert Burns lamented that the castle was a ruin when he visited it in 1787 but the fabric was restored in the 1850s when Britain was gripped by war hysteria in the wake of the Crimean War. Broughty Castle was bought by the War Office in 1855 and given modern gun emplacements to fend off any potential trouble from the sabre rattling Napoleon III. The castle saw further service as an observation post in the Second World War and was only finally pensioned off in 1949. It now houses an excellent local history museum.

In 1440 the Lord High Admiral of Scotland, Sir George Crichton, promised James II that he would 'build a ship that the English could not sink'. The 'ship' that he designed was the grim, squat fortress of Blackness Castle on the shore of the Forth, fourteen miles west of Edinburgh. Surrounded on three sides by water and protected landward by a rock cut ditch and a ship-shaped wall, Blackness appears to be moored to the end of a rocky promontory. The illusion was completed by the large 'stern' tower and the smaller bastion in the 'bow'. From certain angles, the castle resembles a battleship in full sail. Although known by locals as 'the ship that never sailed', Blackness did a good job of protecting the harbour close by, through which flowed the expensive goods bound for the rich burgh of Linlithgow.

The Crichtons fell from favour when James II assumed full power in the 1440s and the castle was 'gifted' by Sir George to the king. In truth, it was too close to Edinburgh not to be in Stewart hands. Although badly burned by an English fleet in 1481, Blackness was one of the most secure fortifications in central Scotland. Far enough away from the Edinburgh mob, it soon became the Stewarts' prison of choice for incarcerating the politically inconvenient. The prison pit had an especially endearing feature. At high tide the freezing waters of the Forth would cascade through an iron grating near floor level and fill the bottom of the pit. Prisoners of rank such as Cardinal Beaton, confined at Blackness in 1543, were housed in the castle's tower and spared the misery of the rushing water. That terror was reserved for the likes of the seventeenth century Covenanters, crammed into the dungeons of Blackness to await transportation overseas. In Napoleonic times, a number of French prisoners-of-war also had the opportunity to savour this twice-daily douche at high tide.

Blackness was strengthened in the 1540s by Sir James Hamilton of Finnart who had studied the latest fortresses in Europe. The walls were thickened to seventeen feet in places with embrasures or port-holes cut for cannon. A covered gun tunnel or caponier enabled the defenders to deal with anyone brave enough to rush through the outer gate. It was held by a French garrison from 1548 to 1560. Catholic supporters of the exiled Queen Mary held out in Blackness after her flight in 1568 and the castle was only won back by the government through intrigue. A formidable structure, Blackness was only taken by General Monck for Cromwell in 1650 after a lengthy bombardment from sea as well as land. In the nineteenth century, it was used as an ammunition depot and retired from military service after the First World War.

In 1018, Malcolm II of Scotland and his Northumbrian foe agreed that the border between their kingdoms would follow the line of the Tweed. Once the kings had departed the scene however, the hard task of keeping the border secure fell to 'smaller folk' such as the Pringles of Smailholm. They were typical Borders gentry and their home at Smailholm doubled as a look-out tower from which they could keep an eye on their stretch of the frontier.

The lands of Smailholm were held by a Norman, David Olifard, in the twelfth century and his possessions were probably defended by a motte and bailey castle. However the earliest records of a stronghold on this site date from 1408 when a keep at Smailholm was occupied by the Pringles, squires to the house of Black Douglas. The current tower dates from the time of David Pringle, laird from 1495 onwards, who marched to Flodden in 1513 and died there with his four sons. Smailholm, well described by Sir Walter Scott as 'standing stark and upright like a warden' was one of a chain of keeps and towers that defended the Tweed valley. Its fifteenth century tower was a simple and plain rectangle; no expense needed to be wasted on a structure that would certainly be attacked and which might even have to be abandoned in haste. Only a low barmkin wall, a stout iron yett and gun loops above the doorway offered any additional defence.

Under a strong Scottish king, Smailholm was safe but its vulnerability was cruelly exposed in times of weakness. After the premature death of James V, Smailholm was attacked by English troops in 1543, and again in 1546 when the garrison of Wark Castle plundered the Pringles to the tune of 800 cattle and 100 horses. Smailholm was far from Edinburgh but close to England. The Pringles had to be ready to trim when necessary. By bowing to the forces of the English Marcher Lord Grey in 1547, the Pringles could get back to the business of running their farms and raising livestock.

In 1640 a skirmish at Smailholm demonstrated the efficacy of the Borders tower house against all but the most determined force equipped with artillery. The tower was occupied by a handful of Covenanters who held out against a much larger force of royalist musketeers. Smailholm was rendered obsolete however after the Union of 1707 as Borders history entered a calmer phase, and it was abandoned in due course. Scott used Smailholm as a setting for his epic poem Marmion and brought his friend Turner there in 1831 so that he could sketch the tower as an illustration for Scott's Poetical Works.

For two hundred years, Cardoness Castle was home to the McCullochs, a troublesome clan who feuded constantly with their neighbours in Galloway. According to legend, they acquired Cardoness through marriage and a tragedy. The previous laird had nine daughters but finally sired a male heir around 1460. To celebrate, he organized a feast on the frozen loch. Unfortunately the ice broke and all were lost except the youngest daughter and her McCulloch husband. A charter of 1466 confirmed the possession of Cardoness Castle in the hands of Gilbert McCulloch and much of the surviving tower dates from that period. Little remains of an earlier motte, held by Sir Nicholas de Cardenes, the descendant of a twelfth century Norman knight given lands by the Crown to act as a counterpoise to the independent Lords of Galloway.

Cardoness was a perfect base for robber barons such as the McCullochs. The castle has been marooned inland by later drainage and land reclamation but in the fifteenth century it sat on a rocky headland overlooking Wigtown Bay and was surrounded on three sides by the Water of Fleet. Six storeys high, Cardoness was in such a secure location that there was no need to build a barmkin or curtain wall. A murder-hole in the south wall and a prison were sufficient to dispose of any unwanted visitors. An English spy in Elizabeth times noted the difficulty that any force would have attacking Cardoness: 'there can no ordinance nor gunes approach it of the sea, nor can any artillery be taken to it upon the lande unless caryed upon men's backes'.

The McCullochs had frequent cause to lie low in their safe tower. In 1509 Ninian McCulloch was prosecuted, and executed, for the theft of fifteen hundred cattle and for extorting illegal rents from local farmers. His son Alexander, known as Cutlar McCulloch, carried out numerous raids on the nearby Isle of Man. By 1600 the family was impoverished and in 1628 the castle came into the ownership of their rival, John Gordon. By 1668 the McCullochs were back in Cardoness and back in trouble. Alexander McCulloch was fined for dragging the dying widow of his Gordon enemy out of her house and throwing her onto the local midden or dung heap. Finally in 1690 Sir Godfrey McCulloch murdered William Gordon and was forced to flee overseas. He made the mistake of returning to Scotland too soon however and was spotted in Edinburgh. He earned the dubious distinction of becoming one of the last to suffer beheading by 'The Maiden', Edinburgh's precursor to the guillotine. After his execution, Cardoness castle slowly fell into ruin.

Spynie Palace in Morayshire was once one of the finest and strongest castles in Scotland. This is difficult to appreciate today, for the physical and political geography that made Spynie important have long since disappeared. In 1200 Spynie was the residence of the bishops of Moray, spiritual princes of one of the richest provinces in the kingdom. In the thirteenth to fifteenth centuries, the tithes from the farms along Moray's fertile coast provided more than enough revenue to fuel the architectural and political ambitions of Spynie's wealthy prelates. Bishop Bricius de Douglas was the first to locate his cathedral, tended by a community of eight canons at Spynie in 1206-7. When the cathedral moved to Elgin in 1224, subsequent bishops were loathe to quit Spynie's outstanding defensive location. Today the palace lies three miles from the sea. In 1220 however, it sat on a headland jutting into the sea waters of Loch Spynie, then much larger and a superb anchorage for ships. Spynie was easy to defend and had good communications by sea with southern Scotland.

The fortifications at Spynie were necessary. Moray was a tempting target to many in the Highlands. In 1390 Elgin Cathedral was damaged and burned by the Wolf of Badenoch, Alexander Stewart, and the palace also seems to have suffered in this raid. In 1460 Bishop David Stewart strengthened the site by raising the present massive keep at a time of great uncertainty following the sudden death of James II. After excommunicating the Earl of Huntly, David wanted to make sure that he was safe from Huntly's boast to 'pull the bishop out of his pigeon-holes'. A stout fortress, Spynie was also a fine home and received several royal visitors including James IV on pilgrimage to the shrine of St Duthac in Tain. Mary Queen of Scots stayed at Spynie in September 1562 en route to her victory over the Earl of Huntly at Corrichie Burn the following month. Mary's third husband James Hepburn also sheltered at Spynie before taking ship for exile and death in Denmark.

After the Reformation in 1560, the Spynie estates were sold off to the Lindsays, making it difficult for later Protestant residents to maintain the palace. When bishops were abolished in the Church of Scotland in 1689, Spynie was left to crumble. Later land reclamation in the nineteenth century drastically reduced the size of Loch Spynie, so that the palace is today marooned far inland. No trace remains of the sizeable medieval burgh that grew up around the palace, peopled by the craftsmen and retainers who lived off the revenues of the bishop. Nevertheless enough of the palace survives to illustrate its significance in medieval times.

In the Middle Ages, the tower of Tarvit two miles south of the royal burgh of Cupar in Fife belonged to the Inglis family. They were confirmed in their lands by a charter of 1487 granted by James III. The basic structure of the tower house was begun by the Inglis family and dates from the period 1550-79. Overlooking the Howe of Fife, the property was usually known as Inglistarvit at that time. In 1611, the property was sold to the Scot family and its name changed to the present format.

The tower's most famous owner was the scholar Sir John Scot of Scotstarvit (1585-1670), a sprig of the House of Buccleuch, who excelled as lawyer, author, and cartographer. Scot is best remembered as the author of a bitter satire on the corruption and venality of the Scottish politicians of the age entitled Scot of Scotstarvit's Staggering State of Scots Statesmen. Rightly remembered as 'the most famous unread book in the history of Scottish literature', the book reflected Scot's patriotic hope that his country's leaders might act in the nation's interests on occasion rather than just their own. Scot had more success in the field of cartography however, involving the Scottish Parliament, Charles II and the famous Dutch mapmaker Blaeu in his project to have the maps of Scotland drawn by Timothy Pont published in atlas form. The atlas duly appeared in 1654 with a textual commentary written in large part by Scot. Scot was brother-in-law to the distinguished poet William Drummond of Hawthornden. Scott and Drummond were both famously visited by the playwright Ben Johnson during his pedestrian visit to Scotland in 1618-19. He also served Charles II as Director of the Chancery and founded the Chair of Humanity at St Andrews University.

Scotstarvit is a classic L-plan tower house on six stories. The tower is particularly solid in appearance, in large part because there are relatively few windows in the tower and those that exist are unusually small. Sir John Scott probably added the battlemented parapet and the pepperpot caphouse after coming into his inheritance in 1627. The garret room at Scotstarvit which Sir John used as a study contained a heraldic fireplace inscribed with the motto Spe expecto but this was removed in the nineteenth century to the nearby mansion house of Hill of Tarvit. In 1780 the tower was sold by the Scots to the Gourlays of Craigrothie and then passed to the Wemyss family. Although unused since then, having retained its roof and having few windows, it has remained in fine condition to this day.

No Scottish king tried harder to curb the power and grandeur of his haughty nobles than James V. To restrain their conspicuous consumption and limit their power to cause mischief, James caused the Scottish Parliament to pass an Act limiting the number of retainers that people of rank could bring with them to the royal Court at Stirling. He was therefore furious when Sir William Murray of Tullibardine approached the royal person surrounded by a great band of supporters in defiance of the legal decree. The king was soon placated however when he learned that the men with Sir William were not armed desperadoes but Sir William's seventeen sons. James graciously rewarded the procreative efforts of the patriotic Murray with additional lands to support the expected offspring of this burgeoning clan.

Balvaird Castle was built in the later fifteenth century by one of those seventeen sons, Sir Andrew Murray, who married an heiress of the Barclays, another old Scotto-Norman family. The Balvaird estates, three miles from Glenfarg to the south of Perth, were probably part of Margaret Barclay's rich dowry. Several prominent coats of arms around the castle courtyard demonstrate the pride of the Scots gentry in their ancestry and one shield bears the worn arms of Murray and Barclay. The Celtic placename Balvaird, meaning 'town of the bard', hints at a long history of settlement on this site which probably included a twelfth century Barclay castle. Balvaird's elevated position on a high ridge was certainly well chosen for it provided distant views over the plain of Eden and the crucial north-south route between the Ochil and Lomond hills.

The castle complex at Balvaird underwent continual improvement during the sixteenth century, ultimately producing a classic example of a tower and courtyard dwelling of considerable power and baronial splendour. The workaday service rooms on the ground floor of the tower are surmounted by a fine hall on the first floor and a look-out tower on the roof. The remains of stables, granaries, gardens and orchard testify to the busy life of a small country castle such as this. In time the Murrays of Balvaird rose to greatness and succeeded to the titles of Viscount Stormont, Earl of Mansfield and Lord Scone. The modest tower of Balvaird no longer reflected their social status and in 1685 the family decamped to the grander pile of Scone Palace where they still reside today. Balvaird was reduced to serving as accommodation for estate workers but had fallen into ruin by 1850.

Royal Strongholds

In the early medieval period, the King of Scots proceeded through his kingdom, living off the hospitality and goodwill of his great lords. There was no single royal centre, although different kings had favourite resting places in winter. Robert II loved the old Stewart castle of Dundonald in Ayrshire perhaps because of its good hunting grounds as much as for its unparalleled views across the Firth of Clyde. Robert the Bruce spent much of his time in later years at the simple manor house of Cardross west of Glasgow where he could be close to the southern Highlands. As the King moved around his realm, so did his officers and his Parliament. The government of Scotland was not yet so cumbersome that it could not be packed onto a mule train.

The Stewarts were the first royals to settle down in permanent centres. They understood the importance of building a strong centralized government and appreciated that bureaucracy entailed secure buildings where clerks and records could be housed. Under the early Stewarts, Edinburgh emerged as the administrative capital of the kingdom and overshadowed the other main burghs of Aberdeen, Berwick and Perth. The presence of the King and his Court gave Edinburgh a commercial edge and by 1450 it had surpassed its rivals. Parliament began to conduct its business in Edinburgh more regularly because the king was to be found more frequently in the castle on the rock. Edinburgh Castle too had become the premier royal stronghold. The royal archives and the treasury were based here from around the mid-fifteenth century, as were the Honours of Scotland, the kingdom's Crown Jewels. The castle was probably the safest stronghold in the kingdom throughout the late medieval period, not just because of its superb geological advantages but because of its defences such as King David's Tower and its early adaptation for artillery warfare.

Although Edinburgh Castle was the ultimate place of royal refuge, it was a cold and uncomfortable dwelling. James IV built a more luxurious French chateau at Holyrood for his Tudor wife in 1500 but that was never more than a pied-a-terre in the Old Town. The real family homes of the Stewarts were further west at Stirling and Linlithgow. Although Stirling had its Great hall and Linlithgow was a palace of European stature, these were both places where the Stewart royal family could relax, removed from the riotous streets of Edinburgh. Stirling and Linlithgow were where the Stewarts spent their most intimate family moments, where Stewart children were born and baptized. Here the Court could enjoy masques, banquets and plays such as Sir David Lindsay's Satire of the Three Estates. In the summer, there was also the royal hunting lodge at Falkland beyond the Lomond Hills in Fife where the most favoured members of the Court could retreat with the king.

Many other castles served as royal fortresses. Castle Urquhart on Loch Ness was an important bastion in the long campaign to quieten the Highlands and bring them under royal control. In the wake of the Jacobite Risings, a string of government fortresses were needed to pacify the clans. The first of these was Cromwell's artillery fort at Inverlochy, built in the 1650s but now almost wholly lost. It was soon superseded by a later network of expensive roads and strongholds. Barracks for government troops were built at Ruthven, Kiliwhimen, and Bernera to police especially sensitive areas. The Great Glen was policed by Fort George, Fort Augustus, and Fort William, all replete with hated Hanoverian names. The greatest of these, Fort George, was the largest and most expensive fortification ever built in Britain and remains as a testament to the fear that the Highland clans inspired in London government. Many other castles in this book were temporarily drafted into royal service to deal with the Jacobite menace. Thus Corgarff Castle in Strathdon found a new lease of life in 1748 as a barracks for a small detachment of Hanoverian soldiers, unlucky enough to be posted to this remote and hostile region. Even Dumbarton Rock, one of the oldest fortresses in Britain, demonstrated its enduring value in this period, with a vast artillery battery added to its ancient walls in 1735.

The rock of Stirling was the key to medieval Scotland. Sitting astride the narrow waist of the Central Belt, it commanded the upper reaches of the Forth as well as guarding access to the Central Highlands. In medieval times, Stirling Bridge was the lowest practical crossing point over the Forth. All invading armies had to come to the rock of Stirling if they wanted to enter Scotland's hinterlands; Stirling Castle was rightly described as 'a huge brooch that clasps Highlands and Lowlands together'. It suffered sixteen major sieges as a result. Legends link a citadel at Stirling with King Arthur but the first records of a castle there date from the reign of Alexander I who died there in 1124. Control of Stirling castle was also demanded by Henry II before he would release the captive William the Lion in 1174.

William regained the castle before his death there in 1214, but Stirling fell into English hands again in 1295-96 when Edward I tried to annex Scotland. William Wallace briefly liberated the castle following his decisive victory at the Battle of Stirling Bridge in 1297 but an English governor, Sir John Simpson, was back in command in 1298. Simpson found himself besieged in turn the following year and called on Edward to send reinforcements. When these failed to arrive, the castle was surrendered and its Scots constable, Sir William Oliphant, raised the lion rampant over its battlements once again. Edward finally arrived in force in July 1304 having crossed the Forth downstream using a fleet of pontoons. At this point in the Wars for Scottish Independence, Stirling was the last major stronghold in Scotland still under patriot control. After three months of siege, Oliphant and his starving men marched out. Edward accepted their surrender but ordered the garrison back into the castle while he bombarded it with stones from his siege engine, the War Wolf.

Stirling was still in English hands in 1314, when it was among the few fortresses not under Bruce control. Failing to take the castle by siege, the king's younger brother, Edward Bruce, parleyed with the English castellan Sir Philip Mowbray. They agreed that the castle would be handed over to the Scots if it had not been relieved by Mid Summer Day. This committed both Robert the Bruce and Edward II to the climactic battle that was fought on the plain below the castle along the Bannockburn that summer. Once back in Scottish hands, Bruce damaged Stirling severely so it could not be held by future invaders. Despite this, after Bruce's death in 1329, the forces of the puppet king Edward Balliol and his sponsor Edward III captured and rebuilt Stirling in 1333, and held it until 1342.

With the stability of the Stewart Age, Stirling flourished. Money was lavished upon the castle, to turn it into a symbol of royal authority. The Great Hall of 1500 and Gatehouse of 1510 built by James IV, and the Royal Palace of James V of 1540, were designed to project the dynastic identity of the Stewart kings. The exterior of the Great Hall was even painted in a bright golden wash so that it could be seen for miles around. Stirling was the effective capital of Stewart Scotland, where the family preferred to hold court and carry out their business. The infant monarchs James V and Mary were both crowned in the Chapel Royal. The baptism of Prince Henry Stewart in 1594 was celebrated by a banquet of gargantuan proportions, even by Renaissance standards. The highlight of the feast was the procession into the Great Hall of an eighteen foot galleon with masts forty feet high from which servants dispensed seafood to the guests. Darker deeds were done at Stirling too. In 1452 James II took the first step towards breaking the power of the house of Black Douglas whose wealth and privileges rivalled those of the Crown. Negotiations between James II and the Earl of Douglas came to a sudden end when the king plunged his dagger into the throat of the magnate. Douglas had been promised a safe conduct but his corpse ended up being thrown out of a castle window onto the rocks below. The Scottish Parliament exonerated the king and put the entire blame for the incident upon the dead noble who had so clearly been guilty of treason.

Stirling was little used by royalty after 1603 but it witnessed blood again in 1651 during a siege by Monck's Roundheads which badly damaged the castle. Its continuing strategic value was highlighted by the devastating Jacobite victory at Killiecrankie less than sixty miles to the north in 1689. Stirling became an important base for the Hanoverian army and its defences were stiffened by modern artillery platforms. More was done to strengthen Stirling after the aborted invasion of 1708 when the Old Pretender sailed into the Forth with a French fleet. In 1745 Jacobite forces bypassed the castle and only fired a few desultory shots at in on their way back north. The castle suffered badly in its years as an army base; the Great Hall was converted into barracks and the Chapel Royal was used as a store. The army finally left in 1964 and after over thirty years of conservation work, Stirling Castle has now been restored to its Renaissance grandeur and magnificence.

Scotland is blessed with many natural fortresses, and of these, Edinburgh is the greatest. There has been a fort upon the extinct volcanic plug of Din Eidyn since the beginning of recorded time. Archaeological evidence shows that the local native tribe, the Votadini, sheltered there in Roman times. The castle enters written history in 600AD in the epic poem Gododdin which tells how 300 British warriors rode out from Din Eidyn's fort on a doomed raid against the Angles of Catraeth or Catterick. The powerful Angles of Northumbria were not to be stopped however and they took Din Eidyn in 638, holding it for several centuries and bequeathing its English name of Edinburgh.

From the seventh to the eleventh centuries, the Lothians were contested lands. Alba or the kingdom of Scotia ended on the northern shores of the Firth of Forth. Edinburgh Rock was only secured for the kingdom of the Scots in 1018 when Malcom II, in alliance with Owen King of Strathclyde, confirmed his control of the lands between the Forth and the Tweed through victory at the Battle of Carham. From that point onwards, the Tweed and not the Forth was Scotland's southern frontier. Now Edinburgh Castle, 'the great safe place of the kingdom', could begin its long evolution into royal castle, palace and government garrison.

Edinburgh's strategic importance was obvious in the landscape for it dominated the rich plains of Lothian and the Firth of Forth. It stood in the way of all invaders from the south. Edward Plantagenet realized its importance to the Scots. So in 1296 he made straight for Edinburgh Castle and having taken it, left the extraordinarily large garrison of 350 knights. It took the skill and audacity of the Earl of Moray to win it back. In the spring of 1314 he led thirty of his men, all skilled climbers and silent killers, up the steep north cliff of the Rock that was thought to be un-scaleable. The over-confident English garrison was asleep and soon slaughtered in their beds. The castle had to be won back from the English again in 1341. In order to enter the well defended fortress, Sir William Douglas disguised his men as merchants and blocked the castle gates with wagons before the defenders realized they were under assault. This English garrison was decapitated and their bodies flung over the walls to the city dogs. Although the Bruce deliberately slighted the castle in 1315, David II strengthened it by building an impressive tower in 1361 that withstood a siege by Henry IV in 1400. Those who saw David's Tower before its destruction in the sixteenth century rated as 'one of the most impregnable castels in all of Christdom'.

Little survives of the medieval castle thanks to the Lang Siege of 1571-73. Although Mary Queen of Scots had abdicated and escaped to England in 1568, her castellan Sir William Kirkcaldy held Edinburgh Castle in her name against the forces of the new government under Regent Morton. As long as the Castle stood for Mary, the Catholic cause in Scotland was not quite dead. The standoff lasted for over a year until a train of bombards from Berwick arrived, courtesy of the Protestant Queen Elizabeth who was keen to support Morton. Within ten days, the castle's medieval defences had been reduced to mere rubble. The collapse of David's Tower under bombardment blocked the water supply and Sir William had to surrender. The religious divide after 1560 added an extra element of hatred to the military disputes of this period. Kirkcaldy's loyalty to Queen Mary was not appreciated by Morton and he was summarily executed.

After the Lang Siege, the medieval ruins were swept away and replaced by a fortress more suited to the age of cannon. Morton built the Half Moon battery that was deep enough to absorb incoming fire and could rake the approach to the castle from the city below. This modernised artillery fortress withstood attack by the Army of the Covenant in 1640 but further improvement was undertaken by Cromwell in the 1650s when his Roundheads garrisoned the castle. General Wade of Highland road building fame built additional gun batteries in the 1730s.

Edinburgh Castle witnessed acts of treachery as well as bravery, none more Machiavellian than the 'Black Dinner' of 1440. The boy king James II was an unwitting pawn in a noble plot to weaken the overweening House of Douglas. The Earl of Douglas was invited to dine at the castle with the young king, only to be served a dish bearing the severed head of a black bull. Within the hour, Douglas had been charged with treason and similarly beheaded. The castle dungeons also held many important and inconvenient prisoners such as the Duke of Albany, accused of conspiracy by his brother, the despotic James III. Albany had the sense to escape from the castle in 1479 by lowering a rope from his cell and scuttling down the face of the Castle Rock.

As Edinburgh gradually became the capital of Scotland in the fifteenth century, the Castle took on a new role as the king's residence. James IV commissioned the Great Hall around 1510 while Mary and her son James VI built and re-modelled the comfortable royal apartments of Palace Yard, although Cromwell later had their ornamental monograms erased from the stonework. The castle also served as repository for the crown treasury, the royal archives and the Honours of Scotland or Crown Jewels of Scotland. The Honours were used at coronations and other state occasions. They were also present at sessions of the Scottish Parliament in the absence of the king. No Act of the Scottish Parliament was legal until it had been touched by the Honours. After the Union of the Parliaments in 1707, they lost this function and were absent-mindedly walled up in the Castle after the Union in 1707 and forgotten about for over a hundred years until rediscovered by Sir Walter Scott in 1818. The Honours are now on display alongside the Stone of Destiny, the ancient coronation seat of the Scottish Kings, stolen from the kingdom in 1296 by Edward I in his desire to eradicate all sense of national identity amongst the Scots. The stone was held in Westminster Abbey but returned to Scotland exactly seven hundred years later in 1996.

The Castle contains two holy places. St Margaret's Chapel is the oldest structure in the castle complex and dates from the reign of her son David, perhaps Scotland's greatest king. He ordered it built to commemorate his royal mother who brought many new progressive ideas from Europe to Scotland and was canonized by Pope Innocent IV in 1250. On the very summit of the Castle Rock is the Scottish National War Memorial, built in the 1920s in homage to Scotland's disproportionate losses in the Great War. Chapels dedicated to the great battles of Flanders hold registers of the fallen. This is a very sad and solemn place where even young Scots born long after the world wars of the last century are moved by the scale of Scotland's sacrifice. Together, these sacred structures symbolize the link between this unique fortress and the history of the Scottish kingdom.

Falkland was a perfect location for the country retreat of the Stewart monarchs. It was only a few miles from the ferries that would carry them to the capital when occasion demanded. Yet Falkland was shielded from the gaze of Edinburgh's censorious burghers by Fife's Lomond Hills. At Falkland Palace, the Court could enjoy falconry and hunting boar in the rich woods of central Fife. Formal gardens with peacocks and archery butts provided other forms of leisure, as did the oldest surviving real or royal tennis court in the world, built by James V in the 1539.

Falkland Palace began as the fortified hunting lodge of the Macduff Thanes Fife, and the remains of a thirteenth century fortalice, destroyed by the English in 1337, have been found on the site. In 1371 the rebuilt tower at Falkland came into the hands of the powerful Robert Stewart Duke of Albany, who incarcerated his nephew and heir to the throne, the young Duke of Rothesay, there in 1402. Rothesay died after a mysterious illness though rumour said that the youth had been chained to a cellar and starved to death.

Falkland passed to the Crown following Albany's fall from grace in 1424-5. James II converted the keep into a comfortable residence for his wife Mary of Gueldres while his next three descendants added magnificence and luxury. James III extended the buildings, spending time there writing poetry and listening to his court musicians. James IV added the Great Hall while James V employed squads of Continental masons to transform Falkland into a fashionably French chateau. By 1550 Falkland was an elegant Renaissance palace that stood comparison with any great house in Europe.

There was little military activity at royal Falkland but it witnessed much court intrigue. The young James V was detained there by his minder, Archibald 6th Earl of Douglas, only escaping by disguising himself as a groom. Despite this, James V loved Falkland, lavishing money upon it and dying there after the defeat at Solway Moss in 1542. His daughter Mary tried to recreate the happy French atmosphere of her childhood there in the 1560s, far from the Protestant temper of the capital city. Falkland's Chapel Royal, although renovated in the 19th century, remains the finest surviving example of a pre-Reformation chapel in Scotland.

Falkland's glory passed with the departure of the Court for greener pastures in London in 1603. Charles I in 1633 and Charles II in 1650-1 paid only brief visits. Cromwell's troops inflicted the usual degree of damage in 1654 when they burned down the Great Hall. The restoration of the ruins was conducted by the 3rd Marquis of Bute in the late nineteenth century.

Midway between the political centres of Edinburgh and Stirling, Linlithgow was the home of Scotland's monarchs. James V and Mary Queen of Scots were both born there and all of the Stewart kings lived there prior to the Union of 1603. It was the most magnificent palace in the kingdom, a fact confirmed in 1539 by Mary of Guise who felt at home in this Scots chateau and declared that 'she had never seen such a princely palace'.

Linlithgow Palace has a fairytale setting on a lochside promontory above the wealthy burgh that David I founded in the twelfth century. The first building on the site was a royal manor of the same period, fortified by Edward I in 1301-2 when he used Linlithgow as his campaign headquarters. To make Edward secure, the royal manor house was detached from the burgh by a deep fosse or ditch and a wooden pele or stockade. Edward's castle was eventually taken and razed by a party of patriotic burghers led by a farmer William Bunnock but the name of Peel is still given to the royal park around the Palace. A second manor house built by the Bruce kings was destroyed by fire in 1424 allowing James I the opportunity to build afresh on the site. The present palace was begun the following year when James constructed what is now the east range. James IV raised the west range which completed the closed rectangular structure of the palace while James V employed the mason Thomas French to add fashionable continental touches. The magnificently decorated north facade was only completed in 1624 by which time the kings of Scotland had been lured south to another kingdom. A palace for living and leisure rather than a castle, Linlithgow had some defences, notably the stout barbican of 1500 that protects the entrance to the courtyard.

After the departure of the Court for London in 1603 a little contingency work was done at Linlithgow to keep the castle in a state of readiness for the King's return. James never made it back to Linlithgow though his son Charles I stayed at the palace during his bad-tempered visit to Scotland in 1633. Cromwell used Linlithgow as a residence during the winter of 1650. Linlithgow was at the centre of great events once more in 1745 when Prince Charles Edward Stewart stayed in the palace of his ancestors. This royal guest was Linlithgow's last. Hanoverian troops fleeing from their defeat at Falkirk in January 1746 took refuge within Linlithgow Palace and started fires to dry themselves and their equipment. These took hold, transforming the magnificent Renaissance structure into a roofless shell.

Castle Urquhart on Strone Point near Drumnadrochit half way down Loch Ness enjoys one of the finest locations in Scotland. Picts defended this promontory in the Dark Ages and there is evidence of an earlier Celtic fortress dating back to the Iron Age. A stone castle was built on the site in the thirteenth century, possibly after the rebellion in Moray in 1228 against Alexander II. After quelling the revolt, Alexander gave the lordship of Urquhart to his son-in-law Alan Durward in 1230 and the wall around the highest part of the castle was probably built at this time. The castle was much extended by the powerful Comyns after 1275.

In the Wars for Scottish Independence, the castle was garrisoned by the English in 1296 but liberated by Sir Alexander Forbes the following year. Edward recaptured it in 1303 after slaughtering Forbes and his starving supporters. Robert the Bruce repaid the compliment by annihilating Urquhart's defenders in 1306. Under David II, Castle Urquhart successfully endured another English siege in 1333. The Stewart kings invested great sums into the fabric of the castle which had evolved by 1400 into a complex and daunting fortification with a double towered gatehouse, high keep and separate citadel.

In the years after 1390, Urquhart was held by the Scottish Crown, not against English invaders but against the might of the Macdonald Lords of the Isles. The castle lay on the frontier between their western principality and the Scottish Kingdom. After almost yearly assaults from 1437 onwards, it was taken by the Macdonald host in 1452 but regained by the Crown four years later. Although the Macdonald Lordship was crushed by 1495, confederations of western clans threatened the castle at times when they sensed the lowland Scots were weakened. Doubtless they sat in the hills and watched detachments from the royal garrison being withdrawn to meet other crises in the south. Castle Urquhart was attacked in the desperate weeks after Flodden in 1513 and was badly plundered by clansmen in 1544-45 at the time of the Rough Wooing. It was however spared the usual battering meted out by Cromwell's gunners, perhaps because it was of use to the crew of the patrol ship that he stationed on Loch Ness. After one small action during the 1689 Jacobite Rising, parts of the castle were blown up by the departing garrison to deny any advantage to their foes. Urquhart settled down to the customary role of an abandoned castle, that of convenient quarry for the local population.

There have been several sightings of the Loch Ness Monster from Castle Urquhart, both during and after licensing hours!

The name of Lochleven Castle is forever bound up with that of Mary Queen of Scots. After her defeat at the Battle of Carberry Hill in 1567, Mary was detained within the small keep that sits on an island in the loch of the same name. Mary was held at Lochleven by order of her half-brother Lord Moray, ostensibly for her own safety, but while there she was presented with her papers of abdication by the Lords Lindsay, Melville and Ruthven, and persuaded against her Stewart instincts to sign them. Constant plotting to rescue Mary finally succeeded in 1568 thanks to a young squire called Willie Douglas. Acting as the Abbot of Unreason during the May celebrations to welcome the coming of spring, Willie plied the castle garrison with alcohol and put all bar one of the castle boats out of action. That night Mary was rowed ashore to a band of waiting supporters and rode off to her final defeat at the battle of Langside near Glasgow.

While at Lochleven, Mary was confined to bed for long periods and probably miscarried during her imprisonment. Most scholars believe she gave birth to stillborn twins who were buried somewhere on the castle island. Another legend holds that Mary had a daughter from her union with Bothwell and that the infant was smuggled to France and held in the convent of Soissons in case she was needed as a diplomatic pawn. Mary's ghost is said to still haunt the castle in search of her lost offspring.

Lochleven was not simply a royal prison. Built by Alexander III in 1257, the castle was taken by the English in 1296. Wallace arrived at Lochleven the following year and massacred the garrison of thirty knights. The English besieged Lochleven again in 1300-1 but it was relieved in time by Sir John Comyn. In 1333 under Alan de Vipont, it held out against the forces of the puppet king Edward Balliol who tried to dam the waters of the loch but only succeeded in creating a pent-up tide that swept their camp away. The Bruce kings stayed at Lochleven when hawking in Kinross but the Stewarts preferred to use nearby Falkland. Lochleven now only saw noble and royal persons who had fallen from grace such as Archibald Earl of Douglas who was incarcerated and died there in 1439. The castle's isolation appealed to the 4th Earl of Morton who lived there after losing power in 1578 until his execution three years later. Well maintained by the Bruces of Balcaskie, the castle remains in good order.

The medieval stone castle at Dunnottar was built in the 1290s by Sir William Keith, Great Marischal, and the only Scottish earl to take his title from his office of state rather than his lands. For over four hundred years, the Keith Earl Marischals had the privilege of overseeing all ceremonial matters at the Scottish Court and were responsible for the safety of the Honours of Scotland, the priceless Crown regalia. The rock of Dunnottar had been a fortress from the earliest times however. A chronicle entry for 681 AD bears the stark message - obsessio duin foither - siege at Dunnottar. The Pictish King Bridei survived that siege by an Orcadian fleet but there were many more attempts to capture this great coastal fortress south of Aberdeen. King Donald II fell here in 895 defending the fort against a Viking host. In 934 Dunnottar under Constantine II withstood a fierce two month onslaught by the expansionist warlord Athelstan of Wessex. With the defeat of John Balliol in 1295-6, Dunnottar fell into the hands of Edward I who placed a large garrison there. The following year Wallace and his men stormed the cliffs below the castle, bursting in upon the startled Englishmen who fled to the sanctuary of the castle chapel of St Ninian. Wallace simply barred the chapel door and burned the men alive. The castle was again under English control in the 1330s when Edward III provided a hundred archers to protect the masons, carpenters and smiths that he had sent to strengthen Dunnottar's defences. Despite their extensive work (much of the present day castle structure dates from this period), Sir Andrew Moray quickly ousted the English.

Three centuries later, in 1645 Dunnottar was attacked by Montrose who hoped to capture the Covenanting 7th Earl Marischal. Failing in this, Montrose vented his wrath by burning every house in the surrounding parishes. Six years later it was the Army of the English Parliament that stood before Dunnottar's cliffs, with orders to snatch the priceless Honours of Scotland, carried to Dunnottar after Charles II's rushed coronation at Scone. After an eight month siege, the Roundheads ripped the castle apart but could not find their prize. The Honours had been carried away by Mrs Grainger, wife of the minister at nearby Kinneff Parish Church. She may have smuggled the regalia out under her skirts, or lowered them in a creel to a maid who pretended to collect seaweed along the shore. The Honours were then safely buried beneath the floor of Kinneff Kirk until the Restoration in 1660.

Dunnottar never recovered from the Cromwellian bombardment of 1651-52. It was however used as a prison in 1685 at the height of 'the Killing Times'. One hundred and sixty seven men and women who refused to submit to the new royal prayer book were herded into the atrocious conditions of the cellar now known as the Whig's Vault. Nine died, two fell to their deaths trying to escape, and most of the others were shipped to slave plantations in the West Indies.

It is difficult nowadays to understand the fear which the clans of the Highlands inspired in the minds of lowland folk in eighteenth century Scotland and England. Today the Highlands are empty and its people have been scattered around the globe. Before Culloden however, the populations of Scotland and England were much closer in size, and as late as 1755 the bulk of the Scottish population lived above the Highland line, speaking Gaelic and owing little allegiance to governments in the south. The clans were fearsome military machines whose men and officers had gained experience of war as mercenaries in Europe. In 1745 a small Highland army under Prince Charlie penetrated England as far as Derby, prompting the Hanoverian royal family to throw their belongings onto barges on the Thames in preparation for the flight back to Germany. The Highlands were a serious threat.

In response, the Hanoverian government began to construct its final solution to the Jacobite menace after Culloden in 1746. The King's Military Engineer for North Britain William Skinner was ordered to commission a fort that would prevent any repetition of the events of 1715 and 1745. The plans were drawn up by William Adam, the architect father of Robert and James. After an aborted plan to build on the ruins of Cromwell's artillery fort at Inverness, Fort George was finally begun in 1748 on a spit of land jutting into the Moray Firth, eleven miles north east of Inverness. The fort was a massive project covering more than forty two acres and with space to house and equip over twenty two hundred infantry and gunnery troops. A thousand troops alone were used as labourers and to defend the construction site. The fort's magazine could hold over two and a half thousand barrels of gunpowder. The fortifications, based on mutually supporting bastions, ravelins and sally ports, were both state of the art and out of scale to any real threat presented by the clans. The final cost was the vast sum of over £200,000, well over a billion pounds in modern terms. The final result was the biggest and strongest military fortification in northern Europe.

By the time Fort George was completed in 1769 however, Highland life was changing and the dream of restoring the Stewarts to their rightful throne had receded into the history books. Jacobite leaders in Paris and Rome had accepted their comfortable lives in exile while their clansfolk were already beginning to be cleared to new pastures in the colonies. Fort George never had to face attack by the massed ranks of the Highlanders although the long Revolutionary and then Napoleonic wars against France gave it a sense of potential purpose. One commander was even reported to have hoped for Napoleon to invade northern Scotland so that the fort's complex fortifications could be put to the test. An army base today, Fort George remains as an eighteenth century time capsule. No shot was ever fired at it in anger.

Ruthven Barracks near Kingussie sits above the flood plains of Badenoch upon a mound of glacial debris, later fashioned by human hands into a superb castle motte. A castle was built here in the thirteenth century by the Comyns to guard the nearby ford over the river Spey and watch the drove roads that made their way from the Great Glen across the Monadhliath Mountains towards Strathspey and the Cairngorms beyond. In the late fourteenth century Ruthven Castle was occupied by Alexander Stewart, the Wolf of Badenoch who sacked Elgin and burned the Cathedral there in 1390. A legend tells how the Devil in the guise of stranger stopped at Ruthven in 1394 and engaged the Wolf at chess. The next morning the garrison lay dead and the castle was in flames.

The Earl of Huntly acquired Ruthven from James II in 1450, and a new improved castle soon stood upon the site. This was badly damaged by Viscount Dundee and his Jacobite followers however during the first rising in support of James VII & II in 1689. Under the Huntlys, Ruthven was usually in loyal hands and the Stewarts could assume that Crown officers would be welcome there. In 1594 however the Catholic Earl of Huntly was out of favour while the Protestant Campbell star was in the ascendant. Argyll invaded Badenoch to press home his advantage over the Huntlys but found Ruthven bristling with arms and manned by the local Clan Macpherson, all armed to the teeth. Argyll passed by and rode on to defeat at the Battle of Glenlivet. The flag of the Campbell Earl finally stood over Ruthven when Argyll's men were part of a Covenanting force that evicted the Huntlys in 1647.

After 1715 the London government planned to destroy the clans by building a chain of fortifications linked by new roads across the Highlands. Ruthven was selected and the remains of the medieval castle were cleared away. Between 1721 and 1734 the old castle was replaced by the current structure, designed to house 120 redcoats and 28 dragoons. Only twelve Hanoverians were in residence however when two hundred Jacobites came calling in August 1745. The redcoats under Sergeant Molloy miraculously held out but were forced to surrender in February 1746 when the Jacobites came back with artillery. The Highlanders duly razed this hated symbol of London oppression. That April, over three thousand defiant clansmen assembled at Ruthven the day after Culloden and vowed to carry on the fight against 'the German usurpers'. Only a message from Charles Edward Stewart, calling on each man to save himself as best he could, persuaded the clans to melt back into the hills.

As in other European states, the early modern period in Scotland witnessed the rise of 'new men' who advanced themselves through trade and business, or as officers of the growing state. Having amassed some wealth and some confidence, these new gentry looked to cement their improved social position by buying land and building a castle. A fifteenth century Act of the Scottish Parliament did much to increase the numbers of these new lords for they were given the legal status of 'tenants-in-chief' or direct vassals of the Crown who owed no allegiance to any other lord. When the property of the old Church was 'distributed' after the Scottish Reformation in 1560, the availability of cheap land and building material swelled the ranks of those who had the means and the aspirations to become lairds. The result was a profusion of new lordly dwellings throughout the Scottish landscape. Most of these new buildings took the form of lofty tower houses.

Whether L or Z shaped, these tower houses of Renaissance and Reformation Scotland were an echo of the great keeps such as Borthwick and Crichton that the greater magnates had built in the fifteenth century. There was in fact a long tradition of building low horizontal manor houses, often constructed in timber, in medieval and Renaissance Scotland. Robert the Bruce had lived in such a humble manor house at Cardross on the Clyde in his retirement years after 1326. Many of the new tower houses of the fifteenth and sixteenth centuries were in fact accompanied by horizontal timber reception halls. Charters by the Stewart kings often required their vassals to build 'a house with a hall', but little trace of these has survived. The enduring image of the period are the hundreds of free standing stone tower houses that are to be found in almost every corner of the kingdom. Earlier Scottish historians sometimes interpreted the profusion of tower houses in Renaissance Scotland as a sign of the failure of the Stewart monarchy to impose law and order on a troublesome population. Current thinking however starts from the premise that tower houses required very careful planning and were extremely expensive to construct. The tower houses of the sixteenth and seventeenth centuries such as Aikwood and Greenknowe were in fact symbolic evidence of a settled state in which the gentry had the time and the leisure to build ostentatious, and in some cases fantastic, homes for themselves. Only rarely did a laird resist the fashion for altitude and build a low level mansion. Despite its undoubted magnificence, Tolquhon Castle in Aberdeenshire inspired few imitations. The Scottish gentry preferred to build upwards.

In some parts of Scotland, the tower house still fulfilled the traditional functions of a feudal castle; to terrify, to dominate and to control. Tower houses were still very practical places in the outlying parts of the kingdom such as the far south-west or the northern isles. Here local lords exercised the powers of a king whether or not they held the title and office of sheriff. The history of Scalloway Castle in the Shetlands is the perfect example of how strong walls could still provide a ruthless individual with the means to tyrannise and exploit the entire local community. Bishop Reid was quick to fortify his palace in Kirkwall in 1541. Even in the heartlands, tower houses needed to retain a full range of defensive features, especially if like Menzies Castle, they were within range of Highland raiders. Most tower houses were surrounded by an outer barmkin wall, strengthened at the entrance with a gatehouse and often furnished with corner towers to provide flanking fire. Corgarff and Braemar were unusual in having a star-shaped outer wall that faintly echoed the great bastions of continental fortresses of the period. The moat or the dry ditch still had a use, while door entrances were usually built at points that could be covered by handguns and muskets. Battlemented turrets provided lookouts and another angle of fire down upon assailants. In the Highlands where heavy artillery was still rare, a tower such as Barcaldine Castle or Braemar was as strong and impregnable in the sixteenth century as it had been in the twelfth.

Standing above a steep bank of the Tweed a mile west of the bridge at Peebles, Neidpath was part of the complex chain of baronial and royal fortifications that defended the border with England. From around 1200 onwards, the first known castle on the site belonged to a branch of the Frasers who served as Sheriffs of Tweeddale. The last of the line was Sir Simon Fraser, a fearless knight and friend of Wallace who entered into three bloody skirmishes against English forces at Roslin Moor in 1302 during the Wars for Scottish Independence. Sir Simon had already earned the enmity of the English by stealing Edward's horses and armour at the Siege of Caerlaverock in 1300. The Fraser champion won all three confrontations at Roslin but ultimately paid the price for humiliating his foes when he was captured at the Battle of Methven. He was taken to London to be disembowelled and executed in 1307. His severed head ended up on a stake above London Bridge, left to rot next to the fleshless skull of his compatriot Wallace.

After Sir Simon's death, his daughter and heiress Mary married Sir Gilbert de Haya of Yester in 1312. Thanks to this marriage, Neidpath Castle passed to the Hays of Yester who held it for over three hundred and seventy years and who built most of the existing castle, perhaps using the foundations of the earlier Fraser structure. The Hays were a family of ancient lineage with ancestors who had served both William the Conqueror and William the Lion. They built well, using greywacke stones and a peculiarly hard mortar to construct the castle's eleven foot thick walls. Originally known as Jedderfield, Neidpath was visited by Mary Queen of Scots in 1563 and by the young James VI in 1587. The Hays were ardent royalists and suffered for their loyalty in the Religious Wars of the 1640s and 1650s. Cromwell's troops besieged the castle in 1650 and Neidpath earned the dubious privilege of holding out against the Army of the English Parliament longer than any other fortress in southern Scotland. The young Lord Yester only surrendered when Cromwell's cannon began to demolish Neidpath's weakest, southern flank.

Neidpath was sold in 1686 to the Douglas Duke of Queensberry and the castle was converted into a home for his son, the Earl of March. Unfortunately the 3rd and last Earl neglected the castles and its estates and gardens, earning the loathing of the poet William Wordsworth who lamented the cutting down of Neidpath's woods in 1803.

At the Reformation, the Erskines of Alloa Tower bought Cambuskenneth Abbey and sold off its stone to local builders. The former Abbot placed a curse on the Erskines, prophesying that strangers would someday own their lands. For good measure, the Abbot also prophesied that an Erskine would see his home and wife consumed by flames. His children would never see the light of day. The curse would only end when Alloa Tower was used as a stable, a weaver sat in the laird's chamber, and a sapling grew from the top of the tower. It took a while but in due course, the curse was fulfilled for the Erskines were stripped of their estates for supporting the Old Pretender in 1715. In 1801 John Erskine watched his residence, Alloa Tower, go up in flames. His wife died in the fire. She had already given birth to three blind children. Dragoons used the now ruined tower to stable their horses, and in the depression years after 1815, a homeless weaver set up shop in what had been the Earl's chamber. Around 1820 an ash sapling took root in what remained of the roof. The Erskines had finally paid their dues.

Alloa Tower, one of the largest tower houses in Scotland, was the ancestral home of the Erskines, Earls of Mar and Kellie. Although the bulk of their estates lay in Upper Aberdeenshire, Alloa Tower was a useful home in the Forth valley close to the royal power centres of Stirling, Linlithgow and Edinburgh. The first Erskine to stay there was Sir Robert who served as Great Chamberlain of Scotland in 1360. Many monarchs visited the castle and the young James VI lived there for Erskine was his tutor and guardian. A local tradition holds that James died while at Alloa and was secretly replaced by a local child. The 6th Earl was a signatory of the Treaty of Union and instigator of the 1715 Rising against the Hanoverian accession. His brother James, Lord Grange, achieved notoriety when his wife Rachel disappeared in 1732. Rachel was prone to spells of insanity and James feared she would reveal his communications with Jacobites in France. Rachel was carried away in secrecy to remote St Kilda. Although her funeral was celebrated publicly in Edinburgh, she survived in various Hebridean bolt-holes until 1745.

The castle remained in Erskine hands until 1988 when the present Erskine, still serving as a life peer in the House of Lords as Baron Erskine of Alloa Tower, passed the tower to a trust for restoration and public access.

The Ruthvens were originally a very shrewd political family. In the Wars for Scottish Independence, they picked Robert the Bruce as the ultimate winner and fought alongside him throughout his campaign. In reward they were made Sheriffs of Perth in 1313 and received a choice selection of lands in the neighbourhood of the burgh to add to the estates they had already held in Perthshire since the 1100s. Ruthven Castle was a convenient base, three miles west of Perth. The castle was in fact two quite separate towers built a mere three metres apart for separate scions of the family. Local legend named the gap between the two keeps 'the Maiden's Leap' to commemorate the athletic achievements of a medieval damsel who was almost discovered in her lover's chamber but jumped back to her own room in the other tower on hearing her mother's approach. Both towers were certainly luxurious enough for a royal romance. Mary Queen of Scots stayed at Ruthven Castle in September 1565 during her honeymoon with her second husband Lord Darnley.

The Ruthvens enjoyed great wealth and royal favour. Lord Ruthven was even raised to the Earldom of Gowrie by James VI in 1581. At that point, he seems to have lost his political touch and the following year he hatched a plot to kidnap the fifteen year old king. After a hunting expedition in Perthshire, James was persuaded to take refreshments at Ruthven Castle, only to find himself imprisoned there for the next ten months. The Ruthvens were Protestant and may have feared the influence of nobles such as Lennox and Arran who were Catholic sympathisers. The kidnapping, known as the Ruthven Raid, proved fatal however for the king eventually escaped and took his revenge upon the Earl who was beheaded at Stirling in 1584. The House of Ruthven had clearly not learned its lesson for a second attempt was made to kidnap James in the Gowrie Conspiracy of 1600. This time the king was not so lenient. Although the Ruthven heirs had already died in Perth during the plot, their corpses were tried for high treason, found guilty and subjected to the full rigour of the law. Their dismembered remains were displayed in the time honoured fashion at Edinburgh, Perth, Stirling and Dundee. The lands and titles of Ruthven were forfeit and their very name was erased from the Book of Arms. Ruthven House was henceforth known as Huntingtower Castle and in due course passed from the Crown to the Murray Earl of Tullibardine. The Jacobite commander Lord George Murray was born at Huntingtower in 1694 but in the later eighteenth century the castle was abandoned.

Preston tower sits on the coastal road to Edinburgh on the edge of Prestonpans, eight miles east of the capital. Over ninety feet high, the lower storeys were built in the fifteenth century using the soft red sandstone used in several other castles in East Lothian. The upper floors added in the seventeenth century are in a lighter stone and a different architectural style, with gargoyles and fine Renaissance mouldings around the windows. These carry the initials SIDKH representing Sir John and Dame Katherine Hamilton who added the L-shaped 'penthouse' in 1626.

The first fortalice on these lands belonged to the Home family but passed to the Hamiltons in the fifteenth century. The current tower was begun in the 1450s by the Hamiltons who had benefitted from helping James II to engineer the fall of the Black Douglases in 1455. Preston Tower's main defence lay in its seven foot thick walls but it also possessed an additional feature; a wooden chamber directly about the tower entrance that acted in the same way as machiolated masonry. This allowed the castle garrison to drop boiling oil or heated sand onto attackers below. An effective fortification in medieval times, Preston was obsolete however when it found itself in the path of the Earl of Hereford's forces in 1544. Hereford simply smoked out the garrison by lighting greased faggots placed against the door and setting his hackbutters or musketmen to pick off anyone who tried to douse the flames. The tower was burned again in 1650 when Cromwell's men were sent to punish the Hamiltons of Preston for sending a squadron of horsemen to the Battle of Dunbar. Cromwell's flames burned not only the tower but the Hamilton's 'charter kist' or documents chest which held the family's most important papers. A new charter had to be issued after the Restoration in 1660. No sooner had the Hamiltons secured their right to their property than the tower was set ablaze again, this time by a domestic accident.

Preston Tower was abandoned after this last conflagration. The prospering Hamiltons of Preston were in any case no longer living in the tower but had decamped to the more fashionable Preston House nearby in 1626. The Tower became a quarry and much of its barmkin wall was cannibalised for outbuildings around the Hamilton's new home. The Hamilton's lost their title and privileges in 1690 when the laird refused to swear the oath of allegiance to William of Orange but the baronetcy and the tower were reclaimed in 1816 by Sir William Hamilton, Professor of Logic at Edinburgh University.

The Castle of St John lies in the centre of Stranraer in the far south west of Scotland. The history of the castle and the town are almost completely intertwined. Before the castle was constructed in or around the year 1510, there does not seem to have been any substantial settlement on this favoured site, on the northern edge of the narrow neck of land that prevents the Rhins of Galloway from being an island. Originally the Castle of St John must have stood above the broad beach at the head of Loch Ryan but the growth of the town and subsequent changes in land and water use have meant that the castle, like Rothesay on Bute, is now a marooned inland.

Stranraer Castle was built by Ninian Adair of Kilhilt, the leader of a 'rising' Wigtownshire family of gentry that had established many cultural and mercantile links to nearby Ireland. Ninian's wife Katherine Agnew was daughter of Sir Patrick Agnew, the Hereditary Sheriff of Galloway. Ninian built a particularly solid three story tower in greystone but a fourth highly decorated floor was added at a much later date. The Adair's new castle at Stranraer was probably designed to further extend the laws and authority of the Scottish Crown over an area that had justly earned a reputation for 'difficulty and lawlessness'. Doubtless the Adairs were charged with controlling not only the local domiciled population but also the transient folk from Ireland who played a big part in the society and economy of the region. As the castle became the focus of administrative life in the later 1500s, Stranraer grew into a sizeable burgh, far exceeding in size its local 'rival' of Portpatrick.

In the 1590s, the castle passed from the Adair family to the Chappel branch of the Kennedys, another significant family in the history of south west Scotland. The wealthy Dalrymples of Stair bought it in 1680. Two years later it housed John Graham of Claverhouse who was appointed to the office of Sheriff of Wigtownshire during the 'Killing Time'. Graham was charged with stamping down on this hotbed of Covenanting and conventiclers, and he carried out his duties between 1682-85 with such diligence and ferocity that he was remembered as 'Bloody Clavers'.

The town of Stranraer, a royal burgh by 1617, prospered in the seventeenth and eighteenth centuries, becoming the market town for the Rhins folk and a busy port for the growing cattle trade with Ireland. In 1815 the burgh council purchased the castle for £340 to serve as its town gaol. When prison reforms in the early twentieth century removed this function, it became a meeting place and a store but now serves as a museum.

In November 1571 Adam Gordon of Auchindoon spotted a golden opportunity to harm his ancient rivals, the Forbes who held Corgarff Castle in Strathdon. Gordon knew that the Forbes menfolk were absent and that the castle was undefended. The wife of the laird, Margaret Forbes, bravely refused to surrender the castle to him however and for good measure shot one of Gordon's accomplices in the knee with a pistol. Gordon ordered his men to pile kindling against the castle door and also light fires in the latrine chutes to smoke out the Forbes retainers within. In the end the castle was burned to the ground. Margaret Forbes and twenty seven of her kinsfolk and servants were burned alive. Gordon claimed to be acting in the name of Queen Mary against the Forbes who supported the government of the infant James VI. This infamous act was however simply another brutal episode in the history of Corgarff Castle.

The tower of Corgarff stands in a wild, isolated place high in Strathdon, defending the lonely road to Strathspey that skirted the northern edge of the Cairngorms, a road much used by drovers, raiders and rebels. Corgarff often found itself besieged by bands of Highland desperados. One gang even captured the castle in 1607, plundering and terrorizing the locality until finally ousted by the Earl of Mar in 1626. Corgarff also found itself the focus of attention from more disciplined warriors. The royalist Marquis of Montrose mustered his men at Corgarff in 1645. The castle was put to the Jacobite torch in 1689 to prevent it being garrisoned by men loyal to the 'usurper' William II & III of Orange. It was a mustering point again in 1715 for clansmen on the side of Bobbin' Jock, the Earl of Mar. Before that year was out, Corgarff was ablaze yet again, this time thanks to Hanoverian torches.

Corgarff's last experience of military action came during the winter of 1745-6 when the castle was used as an ammunition store for the Jacobite army after its journey northwards from Derby. A detachment of four hundred redcoats set out from Aberdeen in fierce blizzards and caught the Jacobite defenders by surprise, capturing large amounts of gunpowder and muskets. The loss of these arms added to the woes of Prince Charlie and three months later tilted the balance at Culloden ever further against the Jacobite cause. In the years after Culloden, Corgarff served as a Hanoverian garrison for fifty men and officers who raised the star-shaped curtain wall and policed the area, trying to enforce the pacification laws against Gaelic, tartan, bagpipes and the carrying of Highland arms. In the 1820s and 1830s, it was again used as a base, this time in the government's attempt to clamp down on illegal whisky stills in the area.

The glory of Edzell is its magnificent Renaissance walled garden and pleasance designed by Sir David Lindsay in 1604 to reflect his scholarly tastes. Carved panels along the garden walls represented the planetary deities, the cardinal virtues, the liberal arts and the seven deadly sins. Niches in the walls were designed to hold flowers, shaped to form the heraldic devices of the Lindsay family. Formal walks were planted and the low box hedging was shaped into the Scottish Thistle and French Fleur-de-lys, as well as spelling out the Lindsay family mottoes; Dum spiro spero (while I breathe, I hope) and Endure forte (endure firmly). The whole complex array of statuary, carvings and plantings created a neo-platonic idyll that was meant to pleasure the senses and challenge the mind.

Not all the Lindsays were scholars. Sir Alexander Lindsay fought alongside Wallace, and Sir David Lindsay stood by the Bruce at the signing of the Declaration of Arbroath in 1320. Edzell, then known as Stirling Castle, came into the possession of the family through marriage in 1358. David Lindsay, 1st Earl of Crawford, took down the old fort of the Stirling family and replaced it with a new castle three hundred yards closer to the nearby Angus hills. Over the years this developed into a comfortable dwelling suitable for the first rank of Scotland's nobility. Mary Queen of Scots also stayed there in 1562 during her military expedition against the Earl of Huntly.

Edzell Castle was never besieged but it was garrisoned by Cromwellian troops in the 1650s. In the 1690s the Episcopalian Lord Edzell swam against the prevailing Presbyterian tide by holding religious services more suited to his taste in the castle's great hall. In the next century, the struggle to make good the family debts came to an inglorious end. The last Lindsay of Edzell was forced in 1715 to sell the castle to the Earl of Panmure and ended his days working in the stables of a local inn. Panmure had no time to enjoy his new purchase for although a Protestant, he was implacably opposed to the substitution of the Stewart royal family by their distant Hanoverian relatives. He went to Sheriffmuir to defend his principles and ended up in exile in France, refusing all attempts at conciliation by the new government in London. Edzell Castle was sold off to the York Building Company which bought many forfeited Jacobite estates at a discount. The castle was badly damaged by government troops in 1745 and by subsequent asset stripping by creditors. The Renaissance garden was fully restored by the State in the 1930s.

The tower of Aikwood in Ettrickdale four miles south west of Selkirk is linked to three names that have a special place in Scottish history.

Aikwood was probably the birthplace of the great medieval scholar and 'wizard of the north' Michael Scotus who studied at the universities of Oxford, Paris and Bologna and served as tutor and adviser to the Holy Roman Emperor Frederick II Stupor Mundi, the Wonder of the World. Michael Scott's interest in astrology and his Arabic studies in Moorish Toledo lent a mystical aura and encouraged his reputation as a practitioner of the secret black arts. As a result, he ended up appearing as a character in Dante's Inferno and Boccaccio's Decameron. Scottish and Italian folklore both remember Michael Scott as a magician and soothsayer able to conjure up demons and command them to carry out his will.

The second great name linked with Aikwood Tower is that of James Hogg, the poetic 'Ettrick Shepherd' who wrote the innovative and terrifying psychological novel The Private Memoirs and Confessions of a Justified Sinner in 1824. Hogg grew up on the neighbouring farm of Fauldshope and listened to his mother's store of Border's folklore as a child. Aikwood featured as a setting for a reiver raid in his ballad The Fray of Elibank while a tower resembling Aikwood inhabited by the wizard Michael Scott appears in his novel of witchcraft and necromancy The Three Perils of Man.

The present condition of Aikwood tower is the result of the care and attention paid to its restoration in recent decades by Lord Steel of Aikwood, the last leader of the Liberal Party and first Presiding Officer or 'Speaker' of the revived Scottish Parliament between 1999 and 2003. In 1989 the Duke of Buccleuch conveyed the dilapidated tower to David Steel and Aikwood was regenerated by a complete but sympathetic restoration that won several prestigious architectural awards including Europa Nostra.

Aikwood Tower's first owner was Maister Michael Scott who received the lands of Aikwood from James V in 1517. The tower was probably constructed in the mid 1530s in response to King James' demand that all landowners in the 'suthern' parts of the kingdom build a defensive fortification 'in these present troubled times'. A charter of 1541 describes Aikwood as 'unam honestam mansionem cum turre'. When the Scotts of Aikwood died out in the early seventeenth century, the tower passed in due course to the reiver William Scott of Harden who married 'muckle-mou'd Meg' in order to avoid her father's gallows after an unsuccessful cattle raid. Sadly, the tower was derelict by the time it was visited by Sir Walter Scott.

The Menzies, correctly pronounced Mingis, can trace their ancestry back to Mesnières in Normandy from where their ancestors moved to lands in Sussex and Northumberland after the conquest of England in 1066. They were well established in lands near the outflow of Loch Tay in Perthshire by 1150, having followed David I northwards several decades before. Two earlier fortresses, Comrie Castle and the Place of Weem, were burned down in 1488 and 1502. By the end of the sixteenth century, the Menzies felt secure enough to adapt the rugged Place of Weem into a more comfortable home, resulting in the present structure which is one of the most interesting transitional castles in Scotland. Part tower house and part mansion, Castle Menzies was built in local stone with blue slate dressings in 1577 for domestic and military purposes.

The Menzies came into their strategically important estates in the mid thirteenth century when Sir Robert de Menzies served at the courts of Alexander II and his infant son Alexander III, rising to the office of Chamberlain in 1250. He played a key role in the negotiations with Norway that led to the Treaty of Perth in 1266 in which the Norwegians ceded most of their territories in Scotland. The Menzies were also an important counterweight to the powerful Comyn family who dominated Scotland throughout much of the 1200s. Sir Robert's services were well rewarded with the lands of Glen Lyon, Atholl, Rannoch and Weem in Strathtay, a sizeable chunk of middle Scotland. A later Sir Robert was a companion-in-arms to Robert the Bruce and a signatory to the 1320 Declaration of Arbroath. Sitting on the Rock of Weem near Aberfeldy, the castle controlled access to the Upper Tay valley and the roads that lead from western Perthshire to the west.

The present multi-turreted castle saw action in the Wars of Religion when it was occupied by General Monck's men. Branches of the Menzies clan fought on both sides in 1715 and 1745 but Menzies of Culdares, too old for the fray, sent a gift of a fine white horse to the Young Pretender. Prince Charlie visited the castle in 1746 on his way north to Culloden and his death mask is held within the castle museum.

The main family line died out when the last Menzies of Menzies died in 1918. The castle found a renewed lease of military life in the Second World War when it served as a base for Polish troops. The Menzies Clan Society acquired the castle in 1957. The society has miraculously restored much of the castle despite the demoralizing discovery of extensive dry rot in 1971.

For centuries, the spectral Bokey Hound was said to dog the Balfour family who lived at Noltland Castle. Legend tells that Sir David Balfour slew his hunting dog in anger when it leapt on him and spilled his wine, only to discover that it had saved him from drinking poison. From that day onwards, howling was heard from the hound's cave under the castle whenever a Balfour died. In 1270 Sir David was killed in Turin while on crusade with Louis IX of France. The dog announced his death to his retainers back home who had just found his strangled wife lying dead in her chamber. The Bokey Hound doubtless has its origins in the traditional Orcadian belief in the varden, a companion spirit in the shape of an animal that accompanies a mortal soul and announces its death with dismal howling. While the hound may be legendary, Noltland Castle with over 60 shot-holes riddling its formidable walls is certainly a grim and forbidding place.

The first castle on this site west of the village of Pierowall on Westray, Orkney was built by Thomas de Tulloch in 1420 but damaged in a siege by the Sinclairs of Warsetter. By the mid sixteenth century, the lands of Noltland were in the hands of Gilbert Balfour who served as Master of the Queen's Household to Mary Queen of Scots. Gilbert was an adventurer who was involved in the murders of Cardinal Beaton in 1546 and Lord Darnley in 1567. Captured in the siege of St Andrew's Castle, he ended up at the oar of a French galley alongside his two brothers and the preacher John Knox. Knox disliked the three Balfours, describing them as 'men without God'. Gilbert was loyal to his queen however and he continued to fight Mary's cause long after her flight to England, rampaging through Edinburgh to little effect at the head of a hundred armed men in October 1571. In April 1572, he stormed past the sleepy garrison at Blackness Castle with a force of twenty arquebusiers but his actions were again ultimately futile. Gilbert eventually fled to Sweden where he was executed for treason in 1576.

Patrick and Barbara Balfour were royalists who entertained the Marquis of Montrose at Noltland when he came to Orkney on a recruiting campaign in 1650. Staunch royalists they sheltered many of Montrose's officers after his defeat at Carbisdale in Sutherland later that year. Their loyalty came at a price for a Covenanter army soon arrived, besieging and burning Noltland in punishment. Although repaired, the castle was abandoned in 1760.

The Brodies held their lands and castle near Forres in Moray for over eight hundred years. The Thanes of Brodie had their privileges confirmed by Malcolm IV in 1160 but their connection with this part of Scotland goes further back in time. Brodie may derive from the Pictish royal house of Brude who ruled in the Moray and Inverness area, although earlier spellings of the name as Brothie suggest a link with brothaig, the Gaelic for muddy ditch.

Brodies fought at Bannockburn alongside Robert the Bruce who granted the family a charter of confirmation shortly before the battle. Another Brodie participated in the bloody Battle of the Park between the Mackenzies and the Macdonalds in 1488. A Brodie scion was denounced as a rebel in 1550 for mutilating one of the servants of an enemy. For a family of such antiquity however, little is known of their early family history for their papers and charters were torched in 1645 when the castle was attacked by Lord Gordon during Montrose's campaign that year. In addition, little evidence survives of the medieval Brodie castle. The present structure, a Z tower house with extensions in the 17th and 19th centuries, only dates from around 1560.

Like almost all noble families in Scotland, the Brodies were inescapably involved in the religious and political difficulties of the sixteenth and seventeenth centuries. Alexander Brodie of Brodie was a convinced Protestant who signed the first National Covenant and in 1640 vigorously destroyed the 'idolatrous' carvings and paintings at Elgin Cathedral. An able politician, he was part of the mission sent to the Netherlands in 1649 to negotiate the return of Charles II to Scotland. After Charles' defeat at the Battle of Worcester in 1651, Cromwell attempted to use Brodie's talents to promote union between Scotland and England, though Brodie was less enthusiastic about the project. Alexander Brodie, Lord Lyon of Scotland in the 1730s and 1740s, had a good Rising in 1745, correctly guessing the outcome and attending upon the Duke of Cumberland throughout.

Brodie debts, accumulated in the eighteenth and early nineteenth century largely as a result of ambitious additions to the castle, were cleared by successful service in India and a lucrative marriage to the Redcastle heiress in 1838. Renewed wealth helped the Brodies to acquire an extensive collection of English, Continental and Chinese porcelain and an exquisite selection of 17th century Dutch, 19th century English and 20th century Scottish oils and watercolours. Ninian Brodie, the popular 25th laird and the last Brodie of that Ilk to live in the castle, died in 2003.

Carnasserie Castle was built between 1565 and 1572 to control the northern entrance to the fertile glen of Kilmartin in the north of Argyll. Its builder, John Carswell, feared for the future as he lived at a time when many expected a civil war between Scotland's Catholic queen and the Protestant Lords of the Congregation who controlled Parliament. Religious conflict had already convulsed much of Europe bringing civil wars to France, Germany and the Low Countries. As the chaplain to the influential Campbell Earl of Argyll, Carswell was well placed to gauge the likelihood of similar troubles in Scotland. Although he tried to maintain peace in the 1560s by communicating with both Catholic and Protestant factions, Carswell prudently bought the lands of Carnasserie from Archibald, Earl of Argyll in the Reformation year of 1560 and set about building a substantial 'place of strength'.

Known locally as 'the heron' on account of his unusual height and stoop, Carswell was a notable Gaelic scholar and translated the 'Liturgy' by John Knox, the first book printed in the language of Eden. Carswell also dabbled in the architectural arts and the castle reflects his knowledge of French Renaissance motifs. In the 1550s, Carswell had served as chaplain to the Chapel Royal at Stirling Palace and had clearly been influenced by the decorative stonework carried out there by the masons of James V. As a result, Carnasserie Castle boasts carvings of a quality seen in few other West Highland residences. Over the main entrance is a fine two-tiered Renaissance panel and the motto 'God be with O Duibhne', the ancient name for the chiefs of Clan Campbell. Bishop Carswell was wise enough not to trust in God alone. His daughter after all was the second wife of Dougall Campbell of Inverawe. Dougall's first wife and family had been tortured and hung by a party of Maclean raiders some years before. Carnasserie was therefore built as a redoubtable fortress in a strong hilltop location with a full armoury of parapets and gun loops.

On Carswell's death in 1572, the castle reverted to the Earl of Argyll and was held by the Campbells until 1685. In that year the Protestant Earl rashly supported the rebellion of the Duke of Monmouth against the Catholic James VII & II. The Earl's rebellion and execution in Edinburgh's Grassmarket was the moment his local rivals had been long awaiting. Lachlan Maclean of Torloisk descended on Carnasserie Castle, sacking and burning the fine house and its policies. It has remained ruined ever since.

A perfect Z plan tower house, the 'tower fortalice and manor place of Claypotts' was built between 1569 and 1588 by John Strachan of Angus on land a mile west of Broughty Ferry near Dundee. John was a typical representative of the rising lower gentry, many of whom had prospered from the growth in trade and prosperity during the reign of James VI. His family had come far in a short space of time for a predecessor and namesake had been found guilty of stealing horses from the Bishop of Dunkeld in 1511. The Strachans may have built the tower to display their growing wealth but also as an insurance against their jealous neighbours, the Grahams of Ballunie. After expensive squabbling over the family inheritance in 1600, the Strachans lost the castle the very next year, having to sell it to meet their debts.

In 1620, the ownership of Claypotts and its estates was transferred to the powerful Grahams of Claverhouse. In due course it was inherited by John Graham, Viscount or 'Bonnie' Dundee. Although a staunch Protestant and dismayed by the Catholicism of James VII & II, Graham was one of many Scottish lords who could not resile their oath of loyalty to the rightful Stewart monarch. When he realized that the Convention of Estates in Edinburgh was preparing to offer the Scottish Crown to William of Orange, Graham left the capital city with his men and returned to Claypotts to plan his next move, only to learn that he had been declared a rebel. He responded by planting the standard of King James at the gates of Dundee and calling upon the Highland clans to join him. Graham died in his hour of victory at the Battle of Killiecrankie, allegedly shot by a bullet formed from the button of a Hanoverian officer. His reputation as a necromancer and a friend of the Devil had led some to believe that he could not be killed with a standard bullet. His lands were forfeit to the Crown. Claypotts passed in turn to the Douglases, the Homes and the State. It is now besieged by suburban housing.

The Z plan at Claypotts was adopted at a number of sixteenth and early seventeenth century tower houses throughout Scotland. Positioning the projecting towers at diagonally opposite corners allowed defenders to fire along the faces of the main castle block. Claypotts was never built to withstand a major siege by professional armed forces. Its function was the lesser one of providing refuge and security against passing bandits or the depredations of a neighbouring laird.

A little inland from the historic coastline of the East Neuk of Fife, Kellie has a long documented history dating back to the twelfth century. In 1150 Malmure, Thane of Kellie witnessed a charter for David I. The lands and original castle were held by Robert of London, an illegitimate son of William the Lion in the first half of the following century. In 1266 these were transferred to the Siwards, a Northumbrian family of ancient lineage that had aided Malcolm Canmore in his campaigns against Macbeth in the 1050s. The Siwards of Kellie chose poorly in the Wars for Scottish Independence however, siding with Edward Plantagenet and losing their Scottish lands as a result. Kellie passed to an Oliphant kinsman of the Siwards who enjoyed the diplomatic immunity afforded by being married to a daughter of the Bruce. Walter Oliphant and Elizabeth Bruce took possession of Kellie in 1360 but preferring to live on their Perthshire estates, gave it to a minor branch of the family. The Oliphants of Kellie built the oldest parts of the castle that now survive including the square fourteenth century tower on the north of the site.

The 5th Lord Oliphant inherited the castle in 1593, adding the central block and the south tower. These Renaissance additions were carried out at a difficult time in the history of Scotland however. The departure of the Court for London in 1603 was a devastating blow to the Scottish economy for the Court was a great engine of patronage and consumption. Minor gentry suffered as the flow of royal posts and favours dried up and the economic recession affected farm rents and estate revenues. The Oliphants were bankrupted by spending heavily at the wrong time and had to sell the Kellie estate in 1613. It must have been little consolation to them that the castle's new owner, Sir Thomas Erskine, was host to the king himself when James VI & I made his only return visit to his homeland in 1617.

Later Erskine Earls of Kellie suffered for their loyalty to the Stewarts. Alexander was imprisoned in the Tower of London for supporting Charles II at Worcester in 1651 while the 5th Earl, also Alexander, supported Charles Edward Stewart together with a small contingent of Fife gentry in the '45, receiving three years in Edinburgh Castle for his pains. Ruined by 1850, the restoration of Kellie owed much to the Lorimers, an Edinburgh family of academics who rented Kellie as a summer home between 1878 and 1948 and ultimately purchased it in that year.

Elcho Castle, five miles down river from Perth, sits on a knoll guarding the Tay and the rich lands of Rhynd, Fingask and Aberargie. For more than five centuries Elcho has been held by the Wemyss family who trace their descent from Gillimichael MacDuff, the Celtic Earl of Fife who held the lands of Wemyss in southern Fife in 1160. Wemyss, pronounced Weems, is a corruption of the Gaelic 'uamh' or cave. The use of this word as a surname may stem from the many caves, some with Pictish inscriptions, that dot the coastline of their southern estates.

The Wemyss' supported Robert the Bruce in the Wars of Independence and in return they received generous grants of land which encouraged cadet branches of the family to flourish. Their possession of the lands at Elcho near the confluence of Earn and Tay was confirmed in a charter by James III to Sir John Wemyss of that Ilk in 1468. The present tower house was probably begun some time after 1550. A local tradition tells of an earlier castle in which Wallace may have sheltered, but nothing of this fortress survives. The earliest surviving documentation to mention the castle, a bill from a local craftsman to the sum of seven pounds for ironwork, only dates back to 1570. An inscription 'EIW' on the round tower of the castle seems to refer to Sir John Earl of Wemyss who was laird from 1622 to 1649 and rose to the titles of Earl of Wemyss and Lord Elcho in 1633.

The family fortunes reached their lowest point in 1745-46. The fourth Earl of Elcho stayed at home in 1715 but the 5th Earl was active on the fringe of Jacobite espionage, travelling to Paris as an emissary of the Stewarts and resolutely 'forgetting' to take the oath of allegiance to the Hanoverian usurper. The 5th Earl's son and heir David raised a troop of elite lifeguards known as 'Elcho's Horse' to accompany Prince Charles Edward Stewart and was promoted to the rank of Colonel in the Jacobite army. He was therefore required to go into exile after Culloden. David's title was forfeited by an Act of Attainder and passed to a younger brother Francis who assumed the name of Charteris, still used by the family. David's acerbic journal covering the events of the Rising reveals his dislike of the Stewart prince and his growing disenchantment with the Jacobite cause. Elcho ceased to be the family seat when the main line moved to Gosford in East Lothian and Elcho Castle was abandoned in the 1780s.

In Reformation times, the tower of the green knowe or 'grassy hill' near the village of Gordon in Berwickshire was surrounded by the marshy ground of the Gordon Moss. It was also protected by a number of architectural features which make Greenknowe Tower, built in 1581, one of the classic Scottish tower houses of the late sixteenth century. An L shaped castle with two rectangular blocks meeting at right angles, the entrance to the tower was built at the corner point where the two wings meet, allowing defenders to shoot at troublemakers in front of the door from two directions. The entrance enjoyed the added security of a stout iron yett that made tackling the thick wooden door an even tougher proposition. Three corner bartizans or turrets acted as lookout towers and their gun loops afforded a safe position for picking off enemies below. A clockwise spiral staircase within the tower gave right-handed defenders the possibility to use their unhindered sword arm to dispatch an attacker below. A low barmkin wall sheltered the stables and storehouses as well as marking out the perimeter of the castle complex.

Greenknowe Tower was built by James Seton of Touch, a branch member of one of the most illustrious family systems in Renaissance Scotland. The Setons were granted lands near Tranent in East Lothian in the twelfth century and despite their knightly pretensions, they appear to have amassed great wealth through their involvement in the medieval coal trade between central Scotland and London. Once rich, they were eligible marriage partners for the noblest houses in the kingdom, and thus acquired lands and houses throughout the Lothians and as far north as Pitmedden Castle in Aberdeenshire. The main Seton estates were in East Lothian and Greenknowe on the road between Lauder and Kelso represented the southern most tip of the family holdings. In the early sixteenth century the castle was acquired by the Pringles of Stichel whose most famous scion was the prominent Covenanter and writer Walter Pringle, imprisoned in Edinburgh Castle in 1660 for his radical Presbyterian beliefs.

Ironically given Walter's devotions, Greenknowe is a perfect example of the new kind of tower house that sprouted up throughout Scotland following the re-distribution of church lands and property at the Reformation. The funds that had once been gifted to the Catholic Church to help maintain collegiate churches, sing votive masses and decorate chantry chapels were now available to build comfortable dwellings such as this fine tower for the lesser gentry.

Although six years had passed since Culloden, in 1752 the embers of Jacobite resentment were still smouldering in the west highlands of Appin and Lochaber. Old hatreds were kept alive by the activities of Colin Campbell of Glenure, the Red Fox, who acted as factor for several forfeited estates in the area collecting rents for the Crown from defeated clans. The Red Fox was loathed for his determination to evict Stewart tenants from their Appin homelands and replace them with his own Campbell kinsmen. In May, as Campbell's horse picked its way through the Wood of Lettermore near Ballachullish, two bullets slammed into Campbell's back. He fell from his horse and died almost instantly. The unknown murderer was spotted escaping over the hills, musket in hand. It fell to the brother of the Red Fox, John Campbell laird of Barcaldine to investigate the murder, collect the evidence and transport witnesses to the trial at Inverary. John, also called Ian Dhu or Black Ian, selected his old rival James Stewart of Appin as the favoured scapegoat. Although almost certainly innocent of the crime, James was taken to the Campbell capital of Inverary, and tried before a Campbell judge and jury. He was hung at Ballachullish ferry in September 1752 and his body left hanging in chains as a reminder of Campbell power in the region. The Appin murder and its aftermath, immortalized by Robert Louis Stevenson in his classic Highland adventure Kidnapped, scandalized Scottish society and is still the subject of fierce speculation.

Ian Dhu was not the first laird of Barcaldine Castle to dispense rough justice. The grim nicknames that attach to its history tell of violent times and desperate solutions. Barcaldine was known as the Black Castle of Benderloch. Its founder, Sir Duncan Campbell of Glenorchy, was feared as Black Duncan of the Cowl. Black Duncan held lands as far apart as Taymouth Castle in the east and Barcaldine on the shores of Loch Creran in Lochaber. Holding these distant estates in a mountainous area of lawlessness took great vigour and ruthlessness. Ian Dhu himself had to defend his estates against a party of raiding Jacobites in 1745 and chased them across Loch Creran in order to rescue some of his kin who had been taken prisoner. With the pacification of the Highlands in the late eighteenth century however, Barcaldine Castle lost its purpose, was abandoned but was then restored as a home in 1896. It has a talented ghost, the Blue Lady, who has been seen playing the piano in the Argyll Room.

The Reformation in 1560 created a real estate boom as unwanted Church properties were 'redistributed' at discount prices. The MacLellans of Bombie cashed in on the boom, buying the Greyfriars convent in Kirkcudbright in 1569 and demolishing most of it, leaving only the chancel to serve as a family burial vault. The convent's stones were recycled to build one of the grandest baronial houses in sixteenth century Scotland.

The MacLellans prospered by serving the Crown. They acted as Sheriffs of Galloway under Alexander II in the thirteenth century. By 1450 there were fourteen MacLellan knights in Galloway, most of whom wisely sided with the Crown in its struggle against the powerful house of Douglas; Sir Patrick MacLellan was imprisoned within Threave Castle and then murdered in 1452 for refusing to aid the Earl of Douglas in his conspiracy against James II. MacLellans were present at the siege of Threave in 1455 that signalled the fall of the Douglas Earls. Local tradition says that in revenge, the MacLellans transported the bombard Mons Meg to the siege of Threave castle in 1455. Sir William MacLellan was knighted by James IV and in return fell at Flodden in 1513. His grandson Thomas also died in battle at Pinkie in 1547. Sir Robert MacLellan served the Crown in a less heroic way, as Gentleman of the Bedchamber, being elevated to Lord Kirkcudbright. Not all MacLellans died heroic deaths. One Thomas MacLellan took part in a riotous street battle in the High Street of Edinburgh in 1526. He ended up dead against the door of St Giles' Cathedral, murdered by Gordon of Lochinvar.

The castle's builder, Thomas, also had his skirmishes with the law, illegally detaining the ship the Jonnet in Kirkcudbright harbour in 1575 until he received a share of its cargo. Two years later he was found to be involved in the lucrative wine smuggling trade. The castle, a very good example of a complete and unspoiled tower house, was built to display his wealth and influence rather than for defensive purposes, despite its castellation and gun loops. It proved to be an appropriately grand setting when James VI honoured the MacLellans with a royal visit to Kirkcudbright in 1587.

The MacLellan fortune was squandered in the 1640s as troops were raised at MacLellan's expense to fight, in turn, for the Covenant and for the King. Cromwell's crushing defeat of the MacLellan regiment at the Battle of Lisnagarvey in 1649 bankrupted the family. The 6th Lord Kirkcudbright was reduced to working as a glover in Edinburgh in the early 1700s. The castle was by then owned by the MacLellans of Orchardton who stripped and abandoned it in 1742.

In 1571, Lawrence Bruce a young landowner of little account from Perthshire had a stroke of exceptional good fortune. A relative by marriage of the Earl of Orkney, Bruce was appointed to the office of Chamberlain of Shetland. He arrived in the Shetland Isles soon after, knowing that he was the only power in the islands, for the Earl seldom voyaged to this distant part of his possessions. As a Scot, Bruce had little in common with the crofters and fisherman of Shetland who retained many of their Scandinavian customs. Indeed he viewed the Shetlanders in much the same light as his contemporaries viewed the native peoples of the Americas and Africa; as ripe for exploitation. Bruce embarked on a career of extortion that made his fortune.

Bruce began modestly, putting his own men in charge of the weights and measures used to assess the payment of dues and rents in kind. His next step was to replace the ancient measures used in the islands with new steelyards and weights of his own design. The island crofters soon found themselves having to pay greatly increased amounts of butter and cloth to the Chamberlain's officers. Bruce turned a blind eye to the sharp practices of the Dutch merchantmen that traded in the northern islands, taking a percentage of their profits in exchange. In order not to waste his own increasing capital, Bruce toured the islands at the head of a band of 'broken men', billeting himself upon the crofters and eating their scarce provisions. Although castigated by a Commission set up to investigate the islanders' complaints, by the 1590s Bruce was in a position to build a residence that reflected his position as virtual ruler of the islands.

Muness Castle on Unst was begun in 1598 as a Z plan castle with an unusually long central block. Bruce knew that he was not a popular man; the castle was studded with gun loops. He needed them for he soon fell out with Patrick Stewart, the new Earl of Orkney, who was determined to level Muness which he saw as an unauthorized affront to his lordship of Shetland. Although family negotiations reprieved Muness on that occasion, the castle was not so lucky in 1627 when it was bombarded by privateers from Dunkirk. In 1713 the ruined castle was leased to the Dutch East India Company who used it to store the salvaged cargoes from the nearby wreck of the Rynenburgh. By 1775 it was roofless and abandoned.

Scalloway Castle in Shetland is a symbol of the tyranny of Earl Patrick Stewart, the most despised figure in the history of the Northern Isles. It was built in 1600 to seal the despotic Earl's control over the islands and their people. Scalloway was then the capital of the Shetlands and the castle was built to dominate the town and the waters around it. Scalloway controlled the main sea route to Tingwall, the ancient site of the Norse parliament and the historic source of the islanders' rights and liberties. Earl Patrick forced the local people to build Scalloway Castle and taxed them to pay for the materials. However the castle's very location added insult to injury for it served as a physical reminder of their oppression by an Earl who had dispensed with their traditional customs and privileges.

The Stewart reign of terror in the far north began in 1564 when Robert Stewart, the illegitimate son of James V, was made Earl of Orkney and Shetland. Robert based himself in the richer Orkney Islands and appointed his half brother Laurence Bruce to act as his deputy in Shetland. Both Stewart and Bruce despised the locals and set about exploiting them for their own benefit. Robert Stewart died unmourned in 1593 and was succeeded by his even more rapacious son Patrick. Patrick was brutal and corrupt. He also felt confident enough to hold both sets of islands under his direct control, building Scalloway Castle on Shetland to remind Bruce that he was a mere vassal.

By extorting every possible penny from his 'subjects', Black Patie lived like a king on Orkney. He never journeyed through his lands without a guard of 'fifty musketeers'. His fleet intercepted foreign shipping to exact tribute, allowing him to build 'sic a collection of great guns and other weapons of war, as no house, palace, nor castle in all of Scotland were not furnished with the like'.

Earl Patrick's grip began to loosen in 1607 when the fearless Bishop James Law took the islanders' complaints to James VI and I. Indicted on seven charges of treason, and imprisoned in Edinburgh Castle, Scalloway's first and only laird was executed in 1615. The castle was occupied by Cromwellian troops in the 1650s but was beginning to need serious repair by 1700. When Lerwick became the new administrative centre of the Shetlands later in the eighteenth century, Scalloway Castle was abandoned and became a convenient quarry for the little building that continued in that part of the island.

In 1714 the last Stewart monarch, Anne, died, exhausted by eighteen pregnancies that had produced no heir. Her disorientated successor from Hanover, the Elector George, was persuaded by clever politicians in London to introduce new faces to his first administration. In Scotland, John Erskine, the Earl of Mar who had been Secretary of State, found himself out in the cold and out of office. Mar returned in anger to his Deeside estates in Aberdeenshire, inviting the chiefs of the Highland clans to join him for some days of hunting and feasting as a pretext for the conspiratorial plotting that took place instead. On 6 September 1715 the Earl raised the Royal Standard of James VIII and III on a small knoll in the village of Braemar with two thousand warriors in attendance. The great Jacobite Rising had begun. It ended two months later with the stalemate at Sheriffmuir near Stirling that forced Mar into exile and ruin.

Mar's castle at Braemar was already semi-ruined before he embarked on the risky adventure of the '15. It had been badly burned in the first Jacobite Rising of 1689. Although roofless in 1715, Braemar was a perfectly formed tower house with a profusion of battlemented turrets, shielded by a low star-shaped curtain wall, studded with gun loops. Built in 1628, it served as a hunting lodge in late summer and as a convenient bulwark against Mar's turbulent vassals, the Farquharsons of Inverey. The castle also controlled the passes of Glen Derry and the Lairig Ghru through the Cairngorm Mountains and over to Strathspey. The fact that the Earl was usually a member of the hated lowland government made this isolated highland castle a target in times of trouble. It was therefore given protection by government dragoons in 1689 after a failed assault upon it by Bonnie Dundee. Undaunted, the 'Black Colonel' John Farquharson of Inverey, a Jacobite adventurer and outlaw who openly lived at his own nearby fortalice shielded by the loyalty of his kinsfolk, took the opportunity to oust the garrison and burn Mar's tower to the ground.

After 1715, with the Earl of Mar attainted and his estates forfeit, Braemar Castle lay partly ruined for the next sixty years until ironically it was bought by a Farquharson in 1732. This laird took no part in the '45 and had his lands laid waste by the Jacobites as a result. After moving to Edinburgh, he leased Braemar Castle in 1748 to the Hanoverian government who set about reconstructing it, using John Adams to repair the upper floors. Perfectly restored today, the castle is haunted by the ghost of a newly married bride who threw herself from the castle tower, wrongly believing that her groom was dissatisfied and had abandoned her.

Aberdeenshire abounds in great baronial houses. Almost all of them are towers like Craigievar. William Forbes, 7th laird of Tolquhon, wanted something different however and proceeded to build one of the most remarkable mansions in Scotland. William had the good fortune, or good sense, to steer clear of the dangerous waters of Scottish sixteenth century politics and religion. His life was relatively uneventful. The surviving records suggest a solid, canny landowner of a kind still found throughout the north east of Scotland. Elected a burgess of Aberdeen in 1578, he busied himself in worthy legal matters, witnessing documents for neighbours and tending his patrimony with great care. He turned up in Aberdeen in 1574 to swear allegiance to the Regent Morton but was probably there under duress and was keen to get home afterwards. For William Forbes was a 'wee lairdie', content to leave the great matters of state to others so he could concentrate on the more serious tasks of managing his estates and improving his home.

The house that William built sixteen miles north of Aberdeen was spectacular. From the fifteenth century Preston Tower that the Forbes inherited in 1420, William extended a new rectangular mansion and courtyard that would not be out of place in the valley of the Loire or the Arno. From its magnificent gatehouse with twin drum towers and armorial bearings to the Great Hall with secret 'laird's lug' off, this is a fine house. William was burstingly proud of his mansion but keenly aware that inaccurate bragging was a cardinal sin in the north east. Hence the carefully correct inscription on the west wall; 'All this worke, excep the Auld Tour, was begun by William Forbes 15 April 1584 and endit be him on October 1589'. An equally precise inventory enumerates William's stock of 'siluer wark, bedding, tapestrie, timmer wark, artalyerie and wther furniture....'

Later lairds of Tolquhon led more adventurous lives. The 10th laird Alexander Forbes fought on the royalist side at the Battle of Worcester in 1651. For helping to save Charles II, he was rewarded with a knighthood. Over-investment in the Darien Scheme, the visionary plan to build a Scots colony in Panama, brought down the family fortunes in 1700 when the scheme collapsed. The 11th laird was forced to sell the Tolquhon estates in 1716 but he refused to leave the ancestral mansion of Tolquhon until roughly persuaded to do so by a platoon of government soldiers two years later. Used as a farmhouse, it was roofless and abandoned by 1800.

Lords of the Landscape 1600-1700

The Union of the Crowns in 1603 had a disastrous impact on the economy of Scotland as the king and his courtiers departed for London. Yet the Union had little impact outwith the realms of Holyrood, Falkland, Linlithgow and Stirling. Scotland was still a separate kingdom with its own Parliament, even if it now had no resident monarch. James VI & I returned once in 1617 and Charles I visited briefly for his coronation in 1633. Charles II used Scotland in 1650 when it seemed to offer a quick way back to the throne but he remained in England after the Restoration. The only one of the final Stewart monarchs with an interest in Scotland was James VII & II but he was overthrown on account of his Catholic faith. In the absence of the king, the Scottish Parliament slowly grew in confidence and power however, while the great regional lairds like the Gordons and the Forbes could concentrate and harbour their resources without exciting the jealousy of the distant Stewart kings.

The first thirty seven years of the seventeenth century were very prosperous ones in Scotland. The country was probably never as calm as when first adjusting to life after the Union of the Crowns. King James in London proudly boasted 'This I must say for Scotland, here I sit and govern it with my pen; I write and it is done, and by a clerk of the Council I govern Scotland now, which others could not do by the sword'. Then in 1637 Charles I misguidedly tried to bring the Scottish Kirk more in line with the ways of the Church of England. His English prayer book sparked a national revolution and a series of wars that was not fully settled until 1690. The Presbyterian Scots who resisted the king's authority in spiritual matters were known as Covenanters for in 1638 they signed a National Covenant, a national declaration of protest against the king's attempts to impose 'a form of English popery' upon them. These events became briefly entangled in the English Civil War between the king and his English parliament in the 1640s. Many castles in Scotland suffered at the hands of Covenanting armies as well as royalist forces under leaders such as James Graham, Marquis of Montrose. Cromwell's brutal attempt to force the Scots into a Union with England followed in the 1650s. Another swathe of Scottish towers was brought low by Cromwell's artillery, and sometimes by his careless garrisons. England soon calmed after the Restoration of 1660 but the very separate matters that had brought seventeenth century Scotland into conflict were not settled by the end of the century. The kingdom simmered through the government persecutions of the 1670s and exploded in Argyll's Rebellion and the Killing Time of the years 1684-85. The overthrow of James VII & II in the English Glorious Revolution in 1688 led to the first Jacobite Rising in Scotland to restore the Stewarts. Where the armies of Montrose had once tramped, men were now marching behind the banner of Bonnie Dundee. Not surprisingly, the castles of Scotland saw more action, and probably suffered more damage, in the seventeenth century than in any other.

The unsettled times meant that great houses in Scotland needed to retain some defensive capacity. In Scotland, the gentry were much slower to move from their old towers into more comfortable residences than was the case in other parts of Europe. Fortified homes such as Castle Fraser and Crathes were fortunately retained rather than being demolished and rebuilt in a more fashionable style. New defensive tower houses were still being built at Craigievar in the 1630s, at Methven in the 1640s and as late as the 1650s at Leslie Castle in the Aberdeenshire Garioch. This last flourish of Scottish vernacular castle-building traditions resulted in some of the finest architecture in Europe, epitomized by the great castles of Mar. The finest of these, Fyvie Castle, is a unique fusion of European baroque mansion and a Scottish turreted fortress. Modest Glenbuchat, equally welded to its Strathdon landscape and a Jacobite stronghold, was to survive into the next century as a reminder that Scotland's turbulent history was not yet over.

The Burnards (or beornhards meaning brave warriors) were an Anglo-Saxon family who held land in Bedfordshire before the Conquest. After 1066 they were reduced to the status of tenants or stewards to a Norman overlord. The opportunity to move northwards with David Earl of Huntingdon when he ascended the Scottish throne in 1124 was therefore very attractive. The Burnards now became 'tenants-in-chief', owing allegiance directly to the King and in return receiving lands at Fairnington near the Tweed. Between 1306 and 1314, no-one fought harder for Robert the Bruce and Scotland than the Burnards. Their reward was a generous grant of lands near Aberdeen that had belonged to the defeated Comyns. King Robert's trust in the family was further demonstrated by his gift in 1323 of the ivory Horn of Leys, symbolising their stewardship of the Royal Forest of Drum.

A little further to the west, the Burnards or Burnetts made their stronghold on an island in the middle of the Loch of Banchory, sometimes called the Leys. This 'insalubrious residence on the bog-bound crannog' of Leys served the family in times of danger for the next two hundred years. They could ill afford to build a better fortress, until their revenues received a welcome boost in the last decades before the Reformation. Thanks to a choice placement of a younger son as Canon of St Machar Cathedral in Old Aberdeen, tenancies of church lands and the profits of other privileges came on stream. There was enough in the family treasure chest by 1553 to begin building a new tower house that better reflected the family's status. The building of Crathes Castle continued apace, although that pace was a slow one and the tower took forty three years to complete.

Crathes had defensive features but, like the other great houses of Mar such as Castle Fraser and Craigievar, Crathes was designed as a home and as a symbol of baronial confidence. Its painted ceilings depicting biblical, classical and medieval characters are one of the treasures of the Scottish Renaissance. Careful diplomacy in the turbulent decades of the Covenanting Revolution preserved Crathes from the plundering and pillage that other great houses suffered. Thomas Burnett was a signatory to the National Covenant but he was also a close friend of Montrose who gave specific instructions to his war band of Highland and Irish galloglasses to spare the lands of Leys. Crathes also avoided the attention of Jacobite and Hanoverian quartermasters in the following century. It has however suffered from ghosts, notably the Green Lady, a maiden of the house who was murdered to hide her shameful pregnancy. Inevitably, workmen are said to have uncovered an infant skeleton at the site of the haunting.

This great baronial mansion, commanding the confluence of the Deveron and Bogie rivers and the road from Moray into Aberdeenshire, has a long, bloody history. The first castle was the Peel of Strathbogie built by Duncan, Earl of Fife around 1180. Duncan's motte can still be seen on the site directly to the west of the later stone castle. Robert the Bruce was carried here when he fell ill at Inverurie in 1307. After regaining his strength, the Bruce went on to crush the Comyns at the Battle of Barra. David, the baron of Strathbogie, supported the Bruce through all the low points of his eight year campaign but made one of the poorest decisions in history by switching to Edward II on the eve of Bannockburn. His lands were transferred to the safer hands of Adam Gordon of Huntly in Berwickshire. Thus began the long association between the Gordon name and the north east of Scotland. In 1506 the castle and its burgh were renamed Huntly in one of the earliest examples of re-branding.

Around 1410 the Gordon laird replaced the wooden fortress with a stone keep. This was burned down in 1452 however in the civil war between the Houses of Stewart and Douglas. The Gordons stood for King James II and had to suffer assault from the Douglas Earl of Moray. Lord Gordon, now Earl of Huntly, retaliated by wiping out the Douglas power in Moray. Now deep within the Stewart system, the Huntlys hosted the marriage of Catherine Gordon to Perkin Warbeck, pretender to the English throne. James IV, a frequent visitor to Strathbogie, witnessed the 'royal wedding'. In the 1550s, the 4th Earl transformed the castle into a Renaissance palace. Mary of Guise was among the first to enjoy Gordon hospitality in their new impressive home. Her daughter Mary Queen of Scots repaid the Earl by defeating him at Corrichie in 1562 and beheading his son at Aberdeen. The Earl himself had fallen dead from his horse in the course of the battle on the slopes of the Hill o'Fare.

The Gordon's reputation for fierce independence and their allegiance to the old Catholic faith ensured further trouble along the banks of the Bogie. James VI attacked the castle in 1594 using gunpowder supplied by the Lord Provost of Aberdeen. A captain in the Covenanting army occupying Huntly in 1640 took exception to the 'somewhat popish and superstitious' emblems that adorned the house. They were promptly 'hewd and broke doune'. In 1647 the Covenanter David Leslie captured Huntly, hanging and beheading its 'Irish' garrison. In December the Earl's guards were shot against the castle walls before the Earl was carried to the waiting block in Edinburgh. Occupied by Hanoverian troops in the '45, the castle was abandoned and became a dump for agricultural debris.

One the great castles of Mar, Castle Fraser near Sauchen in Aberdeenshire is a perfect expression of a castellated Renaissance house. An immense Z plan tower house with projecting wings that form a courtyard, and perfectly at ease with its magnificent natural surroundings, Castle Fraser is among the finest baronial homes of northern Europe. This is fitting, for the Frasers are a Scotto-Norman family of great antiquity. Records point to their origins in Anjou, remembered in the Fraser arms of silver strawberry flowers or frasiers on an azur field. Medieval Frasers who held lands in Tweeddale, East Lothian and Stirlingshire played a prominent part in the Wars for Scottish Independence, none more so than the great champion Sir Simon Fraser who shared the same barbaric fate as his friend William Wallace. In the later medieval period, branches of the family resettled further north; the Lovat Frasers entrenched themselves within Beaufort Castle near Beauly while the Frasers of Philorth moved to the north east in 1375.

A minor branch of the complex Fraser family system, the Donside lairds of Castle Fraser trace their ancestry from Sir Alexander Fraser of Cornton, who fought alongside Robert the Bruce at the Battle of Methven in 1306 and was captured and executed in the field. Thomas Fraser of Cornton resigned his Stirlingshire lands to James II in the mid fifteenth century in exchange for estates in Aberdeenshire. The Frasers of Muchall steered a tortuous path through the difficult politics of Scotland in the seventeenth and eighteenth centuries. The third Baron Fraser was a zealous Covenanter who entertained Montrose within the castle. Later, in his royalist phase, Montrose twice threatened Castle Fraser. The fourth laird was a dedicated Jacobite. His stepson, Charles Fraser of Inverallochy, led his men at Culloden but was captured and shot by specific order of Butcher Cumberland.

Originally known as the Castle of Muchil-in-Mar, Castle Fraser was begun around 1455 upon Thomas' arrival in the north east but his early keep was absorbed in 1575 within a larger Z tower commissioned by Michael Fraser of Stoneywood. These ambitious works were only finished in 1636 by his son Andrew, created Lord Fraser in 1633 by Charles I. The great mason, John Bell, who worked on the other masterpieces of Mar at Craigievar, Crathes and Midmar, was responsible for much of the final work here. The castle with its profusion of turrets, decorative stone cannon, battlements, and balustraded great round tower has had little need of its defenses.

'*Nothing on arth remanis bot fame John Gordone*' - *Helen Carnegie 1590*. So reads the inscription on this well-preserved tower house above the junction of the Water of Buchat and the glorious river Don. John Gordon of Cairnbarrow built the castle as a residence for his new wife Helen, the daughter of Sir Robert Carnegie, ambassador to the French Court. Despite its setting in Strathdon on the edge of the Highland line, continental influences are apparent in the architecture of lonely Glenbuchat such as the flying arches supporting the stair turrets, a device popular in sixteenth century France. The philosophy in the lintel inscription is homespun however, expressing one strand in the laconic worldview of the folk of north-east Scotland.

At least one of John and Helen's descendants got the point. In the first half of the eighteenth century, the Laird of Glenbuchat earned eternal fame for his loyalty to the Stewarts and his implacable hostility to the German usurpers. John Gordon, Old Glenbucket, acquired a legendary status as the avenging angel of Jacobitism that was out of proportion to his rank as a modest upland laird. Although a man of little property, he was respected throughout the Highlands and feared by Government troops. George II was haunted in his dreams by an image of the great highland warrior and heard to dribble in broken English 'Der gread Glenboggat is kommin'. The Earl of Mar consulted with Old Glenbucket before raising the Standard of King James and sparking the 1715 Rising. As a youth, Glenbuchat was out in 1689 with Bonnie Dundee and led the battalion of Gordons at Sheriffmuir in 1715. Although in his late seventies by 1746, he appeared at the head of his men at Culloden, sitting on a grey Highland pony. In the desperate days after the battle, as Butcher Cumberland's men cut a bloody swathe through the villages of the defeated clans, this unbowed soul met with Lovat and Lochiel at Loch Arkaig, planning to raise new battalions and re-launch the Rising. Finally persuaded to leave Scotland on a Swedish sloop, he ended up in France and died in Boulougne in 1750, taking pride in his specific exemption from the London government's Act of Indemnity of 1747.

Alas, although John won lasting renown for his house, most of his estates in Glenbuchat had been sold in 1738 to raise money for the Rising. The rest of the Glenbuchat lands were forfeit in 1746 and the castle was soon abandoned. The ruins were stabilized by a thoughtful landlord James Barclay in 1901.

Danzig Willie, the merchant William Forbes, made his money from Aberdeen's rich trade with the lands of the Baltic Sea. Willie sent fish and woollen goods to the cities of northern Germany and brought back timber in return. His business prospered and Willie invested much of his money in a fine tower house in Strathdon begun by the bankrupt Mortimers. Between 1610 and its completion in 1626, Willie lavished money and attention on Craigievar Castle, employing the distinguished master mason John Bell. The partnership between the well-travelled and educated merchant and the gifted, experienced mason had a happy result. Although one of the last tower houses built in Scotland, it is without question the finest. A synthesis of the best of the vernacular tradition with continental influences, it has rightly been described as 'claiming a Scottish place in the front ranks of European architecture'.

Six stories high in pink granite, the slender shaft of Craigievar has mythic, romantic qualities. It also has defensive ones and needed them; the castle staff had to repulse a raid by Highland opportunists in the 1640s. The lower stories originally had few windows and the castle door was protected by an iron yett. The castle precinct was also enclosed within a barmkin wall with towers at the angles. In contrast to the stark lower walls however, the upper reaches are a riot of corbelling and ornament. Through good fortune, Craigievar escaped later improvements and so it remains an untouched Jacobean baronial home inside. The plaster ceiling of the Great Hall displays the heraldic arms of Willie Forbes and those of his wife Margaret Woodward. Medallions illustrate a range of mythical, historical and Biblical figures such as Hector of Troy and Alexander the Great.

Willie Forbes had precious little time to enjoy his architectural jewel for he died one year after its completion. His son was made a Baronet of Nova Scotia in 1630, and was swept up by the great events of the next two decades, capturing Harthill Castle near Bennachie in 1640 before being captured himself at the Battle of Aberdeen in 1644. Sir John Forbes the 7th Baronet deserves special mention. In 1823 he realized that Craigievar was in need of repair. Rather than adding newer, more fashionable wings, Sir John repaired the castle without amendment. This astute tribute to the vision of Danzig Willie and his master mason is one of the earliest cases in Scotland where a building was preserved for its aesthetic and historic value.

A Jacobean palace rather than a strongpoint, Fyvie Castle in Aberdeenshire sits above the river Ythan. In medieval times when Fyvie was a true fortress, the river meandered around it creating impenetrable marches. Originally a royal lodge, by the thirteenth century a great curtain wall created a square courtyard almost fifty metres wide. William the Lion held a parliament here in 1214. Other royal visitors included the welcome Alexander II in 1222 and the unwelcome Edward I in 1296. Bruce stayed here in 1308 during 'the herschip' or harrying of Buchan, his campaign to crush his Comyn enemies. Montrose occupied the castle in 1644 and it was garrisoned by Roundheads in the 1650s.

Fyvie passed from Crown to Lindsay hands in 1380 but seventeen years later it was a Preston stronghold. The Prestons were the first of five families to leave their mark on the existing structure, heightening the walls and corner towers, one of which survives as the Preston Tower at the east end of the southern facade. Sir Alexander Meldrum constructed his tower at the western end in the fifteenth century. The Setons made the deepest impression upon Fyvie, building the twin drum towers and high central arch over the entrance. They were outlawed in 1690 for their Jacobite loyalties and succeeded by the Gordon Earls of Aberdeen who built the north tower. Alexander Forbes-Leith, who made his money in the Illinois Steel Company, bought Fyvie in 1885 for £175,000, adding his own tower five years later.

The Ythan that flows by Fyvie Castle was once known as the 'the richest rig in Scotland'. The largest pearl in the Crown of Scotland was found in it near Fyvie and presented to James VI in 1620. As befits a palace of this size, Fyvie has mysterious phenomena. The Green Lady is the shade of Lilias Drummond, chatelaine of Fyvie, starved to death by her husband in 1601. When he remarried soon after her death, Lilias returned to scratch her name on the windowsill of the bedchamber being used by the laird and his new bride. The Grey Lady began to make her presence felt in the 1920s when a skeleton was found in the castle walls by workmen and interred in the local kirkyard. Her haunting ceased when the bones were returned to their resting place within the castle. The castle is cursed; the laird will die and his wife lose her sight should he enter the secret chamber below the castle's Charter Room.

Beautiful Ballindalloch Castle, the Pearl of the North, owes its existence to a helpful dream. The laird of Ballindalloch had begun to build his castle on a nearby hill above Bridge of Avon. When his new structure was blown down in a storm, the laird heard an internal voice telling him to build instead in the low-lying riverside coo-haugh. Ballindalloch's romantic location by the confluence of the Spey and Avon was the result. Later owners may have regretted the laird's change of plan for Ballindalloch was badly damaged by the Muckle Spate or great flood of 1829.

The powerful Clan Grant built the Z plan core of Ballindalloch Castle in the sixteenth century; in 1546 in fact, if a stone lintel is to be believed. The original castle needed substantial repair after James Graham, Marquis of Montrose, passed by following the Battle of Inverlochy in 1645. Montrose left his personal calling card, badly damaging the castle and plundering the surrounding farms. Ballindalloch had been an effective enough redoubt in the perennial feuding between the Grants and their Gordon neighbours but Montrose had artillery as well as experienced men skilled in picking a baronial estate clean.

The transformation of Ballindalloch Castle from tower house into magnificent Scots baronial mansion was begun by General James Grant in the 1770s when he returned from the rebellion in the American colonies. Grant, an effective soldier and successful governor of East Florida, was infuriated by the incompetence of his aristocratic superiors. On his return to Strathspey, he became famed for his hospitality. He built two domestic wings, one for the private use of his French chef. He bequeathed the castle to his nephew Macpherson of Invereshie who in 1838 assumed the surname Macpherson-Grant, thus uniting the two great clan names of Strathspey.

Ballindalloch is home to one of the oldest cattle herds in the world. The estate's Aberdeenshire-Angus cattle have been developed from beasts bought in 1860 from the famous agriculturalist William McCombie of Tillyfour, who preserved and improved the breed. It also houses one of the finest collections of seventeenth century Spanish paintings in private hands. The castle is also visited by four spectres. A young woman haunts the Pink Tower while a green lady occupies in the dining room. A love-lorn apparition has been seen posting her unanswered letters at Old Avon Bridge while the shade of General Grant has frequently been spotted going down to the castle cellars, presumably in search for the other spirits for which Strathspey is famous.

Lethington Castle near Haddington in East Lothian was the seat of the Maitlands, a Norman family who participated in the Conquest of England in 1066. Thomas Maitland served William the Lion while Sir Richard Maitland acquired estates in the Borders during the reign of Alexander III. His patriotic son William supported Robert the Bruce but died in 1315. Robert Maitland received the lands of Ledingtoune in 1345 but had little time to enjoy them before his death at Neville's Cross the following year. The Maitlands later acquired tracts of rich land such as the Barony of Curry near Edinburgh but they certainly earned them. Robert Maitland held the politically sensitive post of Constable of Dunbar Castle, the important royal fortress in East Lothian, while his son was one of the hostages sent to London in return for the liberation of James I in 1424.

Upon acquiring Ledingtoune or Letherington Castle in 1345, the Maitlands embarked on rebuilding and strengthening program. Nevertheless, the castle needed repairs once again in 1549 after the English burned it to the ground. The Maitlands could easily afford the bill for they held some of the great offices of state in the sixteenth century. The lawyer, poet and historian Sir Richard Maitland served as Keeper of the Privy Seal. His son William was the confidante of Mary Queen of Scots and helped arrange her escape from Lochleven Castle in 1568. Later Maitlands rose to the titles of Earl, and briefly, Duke of Lauderdale.

The castle was given its new name of Lennoxlove in the eighteenth century when Lord Blantyre bought the Lethington estates. Blantyre had been left his fortune by an aunt, Frances Teresa Stewart, Duchess of Richmond and Lennox. She was an outstanding beauty at the court of Charles II and although the merry monarch was 'mighty hot upon her', she connected with the Duke of Richmond instead, or perhaps as well. Frances was the model for the figure of Britannia that featured on the coinage of Great Britain from 1667 until decimalisation in 1971. Letherington Castle was renamed Lennoxlove in her honour. In 1947 the castle passed to the Dukes of Hamilton who have used it as their family seat ever since. It contains memorabilia of the first flight over Everest by the Marquis of Clydesdale in April 1933, and of his later encounter as Duke of Hamilton with Rudolph Hess who flew to Scotland in 1941 to try and negotiate a peace with Britain. The house also contains the death mask of Mary Queen of Scots as well as the casket that may have contained the incriminating letters that sealed her fate in 1584.

The present Scone Palace is a recent construction, a fine Gothic Revival mansion built in 1802 by William Atkinson who later designed Abbotsford for Sir Walter Scott. However this elegant nineteenth century house incorporates part of an older, fortified dwelling built in the 1580s by the ambitious Ruthven family. The lands of Scone came to the present Murray owners after 1600 when the Ruthvens fell from royal favour with the failure of the Gowrie Conspiracy.

Traces of a legionary marching camp show that Scone's location on the very edge of the known world had military value in Roman times. By 600 it was the capital of a small Pictish kingdom. When the Picts converted from their beliefs in water spirits, Scone became a centre of Christian activity. Celtic holy men, the Culdees, established a community of monks there before 700. This prestigious institution was only superseded more than four hundred years later with the foundation of an Augustinian abbey by Alexander I in 1114. The abbey and the bishop's palace that stood on the site of the present house were eventually sacked by a Protestant mob in 1559 after an especially rousing sermon by John Knox in nearby Perth.

Scone took centre stage in Scottish politics in the late 8th and 9th centuries when the Vikings burst upon the ancestral lands of the Scots in the West. The Kingdom of the Scots began to look eastwards for new lands that were safer from the Norse threat. The first great King of Scots, Kenneth MacAlpin, absorbed the Pictish kingdom of Scone in the 830s. A legend tells how he invited the unsuspecting Pictish king Drostan and his nobles to a banquet at Scone where they were wined, dined and slaughtered. It is believed that soon after this MacAlpin brought the Stone of Destiny, used for the inauguration of the Kings of Scots, to Scone.

The presence of the Stone of Destiny made Scone one of the most important locations in Scotland throughout the early medieval period. Ten Scottish Parliaments were held there between 1284 and 1401 while the ringing of the great bell of Scone Abbey marked the promulgation of each new law. In 1306, Robert the Bruce hurried to Scone to legitimise his bid for power after slaying his Comyn rival in Dumfries High Kirk. Although Bruce sat upon the Stone of Destiny, a thin golden circlet had to deputise for the Scottish crown. In the absence of the Earl of Buchan who had the right to place the crown upon the King of Scots, Isobel, Countess of Buchan and Bruce's sister, played her husband's part. The last coronation at Scone; that of Charles II in 1651 was not as rushed. The only Presbyterian coronation in British history, the sermon alone lasted over an hour and a half. Later Murrays of Scone paid for their loyalty to the true kings of Scotland. The 5th and 6th Viscounts were imprisoned for their hospitality to the Old and Young Pretenders in 1715 and 1745.

According to Burke's Peerage, the Scottish house of Leslie can trace their ancestry to Attila the Hun. A Hungarian nobleman by the name of Bartolf accompanied St. Margaret to the court of Malcolm Canmore in 1069. Malcolm was impressed by Bartolf and appointed him as Constable of Edinburgh Castle. Bartolf also impressed the king's sister Beatrix who subsequently married him and brought as her dowry, the lands and wooden fortress of Lesslyn; later Leslie, near Aberdeen. Their son Malcolm became castellan of the royal fortress at Inverurie while their great-grandson gained lands in Fife, now also called Leslie.

The Leslie family divided into separate branches which all had an impact upon Scottish and European history. Sir Norman Leslie attended Bruce's great Parliament in 1314 while his son Andrew signed the Declaration of Arbroath in 1320. The descendants of Sir Andrew Leslie rose to be Earls of Ross and Rothes. The Aberdeenshire Leslies of Balquhain near Bennachie spawned ten distinct baronial houses in Scotland and Ireland, as well as Leslie Counts in France, Russia, and Germany. Six Leslies fell at the Battle of Harlaw in 1411 and several died at Flodden. George Leslie witnessed the marriage of the Mary Queen of Scots to the French Dauphin in 1558. Other Leslies excelled as soldiers. Alexander Leslie of Balgonie fought for Gustavus Adolphus of Sweden before returning home to command the Covenant Army at Marston Moor in 1644. Another Alexander Leslie became Governor of Smolensk. John Leslie of Rothes defeated Montrose at Philiphaugh in 1645.

The barony of Leslie and the castle remained in the family until 1620 when through a combination of marriage and mortgage, it passed to the rival Aberdeenshire family of Forbes. William Forbes of Leslie repaired the castle in 1651 and proudly placed his coat of arms above the entrance. Even at this late date, Leslie Castle was given a moat, an outer defensive barmkin wall, a gatehouse and a drawbridge. Although baronial houses in central and southern Scotland were becoming residences rather than castles, Leslie was too close to the Highland line with the possibility of raiders coming down from Strathdon, to be left undefended. However Leslie Castle was to be one of the last fortified towers for the political atmosphere of Scotland, even in Upper Aberdeenshire, was changing. As the need for heavily defensive structures diminished Leslie Castle was abandoned in the nineteenth century and the castle fell into ruin. It was rescued in the later twentieth century by the sympathetic restoration carried out by new owners, the architect David Leslie and his wife Leslie. It is now one of the few tower houses that are still lived in as a home.

Leslie Castle is a private home and is not open to the public.

Palaces of Prosperity 1700-1900

In March 1746, the Jacobite commander Lord George Murray besieged Blair Castle in Perthshire in an attempt to winkle out the Hanoverian garrison inside. This unsuccessful action was the very last siege in Britain. A few weeks later, the moors of Culloden witnessed the last battle fought on British soil. With the passing of the Jacobite threat, calm descended upon most of Scotland. The Pacification Acts banning the very symbols of the Highland military life; tartan, bagpipes and the claymore; were met with virtually no resistance. Within a few years, the Clearances were well under way as the clansfolk left for better prospects in the Americas. Others took the King's shilling and left their glens wearing the new approved regimental tartans to fight for the British Empire. Most ended up as cheap labour in the mills of the Central Belt. The net result was a peace throughout much of Scotland that ended hundreds of years of bloody conflict. Even in the wildest Highland glen, the age of castles was brought to an end.

Thirlestane, a stately home rather than a castle proper, had been one of the first signs that Scotland was entering a new political and architectural age. Built in the 1670s for the Duke of Lauderdale, Charles II's governor in Scotland, Thirlestane Castle was a fortification in name only. In reality it was a fine baroque mansion with picturesque baronial decoration. At Floors Castle near Kelso, the Duke of Roxburghe built a Palladian villa that might have graced the banks of the Tiber or Arno. Its location directly opposite the crumbling remains of Roxburgh Castle, once the mightiest fortress in southern Scotland, only emphasised that Scotland had entered an entirely new phase in its history. The Jacobite adventures were merely a brief distraction from the serious business of Trade, Union and Empire that now occupied the attention of Scotland's ruling elites.

After centuries of stubbornly defending their national independence, in the eighteenth century most Scots became enthusiastic Britons, throwing themselves into the modernizing spirit of the age. The very name of Scotland seemed to reek of the primitive and medieval and some preferred to call themselves North Britons rather than Scots. Nothing was more redolent of the old 'backward' Scotland than her heritage of hundreds of crumbling towers and fortresses. Most were abandoned; some were deliberately dismantled while almost all were a convenient quarry for builders in search of ready cut stone. The fate of Kincardine Castle south of Aberdeen was instructive. In the Middle Ages it had been one of the largest fortresses in Scotland and the seat of the King's Court and his Parliament on many occasions. During the agricultural improvements of the eighteenth and nineteenth centuries, a new purpose was found for every one of Kincardine's stones. The castle completely disappeared, transformed into hundreds of cottages, byres, stables and dykes throughout the farmlands of Angus. Scotland's history and identity were under a very similar threat.

It fell to Sir Walter Scott, a unique hybrid of romantic Tory and scholarly Nationalist, to save Scotland's history and its castle monuments. Scott's powerful historical novels re-awakened the Scottish sense of national identity and rekindled an interest in the nation's heritage. In the 1830s and 1840s, paddle steamers and then trains allowed the southern masses to visit the wild places of Scotland for themselves for the first time. Mass tourism was born in the Trossachs as thousands came to relive the Waverley novels. Victoria and Albert were part of the romantic nineteenth century fascination with all things Scottish and especially all things Highland. Their decision to summer each year in Scotland and build a new castle at Balmoral sparked a thousand Scots Baronial imitations that can be seen in every holiday town and village. The fashion for Scottish history also saved many crumbling towers from further deterioration as new southern owners of Highland estates shored up the 'Gothic' ruins that added atmosphere and a sense of mystery to the landscape. Victoria was especially keen to preserve and continue Highland heritage. Exactly one hundred years to the day after Lord George Murray took command of the Jacobites, she presented her colours to the ceremonial Highland army of the Atholl Highlanders at Blair Castle.

Blair Castle controls Strath Garry in the very heart of Scotland, guarding the routes through to the Cairngorms and north to Inverness. For more than seven hundred years, Blair has belonged to the Earls and Dukes of Atholl. The first castle was erected by the Comyns of Badenoch in 1269 but the Earls of Atholl took exception to this incursion upon their lands. Once the Comyns had been evicted, the Atholls moved in and have stayed there ever since. The original Comyn tower survives in part and has been absorbed into the complex structure that survives today.

The Earldom of Atholl passed to the Stewarts of Balvenie in the 1450s as a reward for their efforts against the Douglases and the Macdonalds. Life afterwards was remarkably peaceful given Blair's crucial location until the Wars of Religion in the seventeenth century. In the 1640s the Earl and his heir were monarchists which resulted in a column of Roundheads marching up the road from Perth to Blair Atholl. The castle was taken in 1652 and held by Cromwell until 1660. The loyalty of the Atholls to the Stewarts was rewarded however and they rose to the rank of Duke of Atholl in 1703. The new Duke was strongly against the proposed union of the Scottish and English parliaments and steadfastly refused the inducements from London to change his mind. For his pains, he was put under house arrest in 1708 until the tension in Scotland that followed the unpopular Treaty of Union settled down. Like many Highland families, the Atholls were divided in Jacobite times. The Duke supported the London government while his Jacobite heir went into exile in 1715, returning with Prince Charles as one of the Seven Men of Moidart thirty years later. The last siege in Britain took place at Blair Castle in the 1745 Rising. The castle had been occupied by Hanoverian troops and was unsuccessfully besieged by Jacobite forces in March 1746 on their way north to Culloden.

Mary Queen of Scots stayed at Blair in August 1564 and took part in a Highland hunt in Glen Tilt. Over three thousand clansmen drove the wildlife from the surrounding glens towards the hunters who managed to bag three hundred and sixty deer and five wolves. Victoria and Albert stayed at the castle in 1842 and 1844, protected by a bodyguard of a hundred specially chosen Atholl Highlanders. Victoria was so impressed by this body of men that she presented them with regimental colours. The Atholl Highlanders remain the only private army permitted in Britain.

Thirlestane Castle is a fine Stewart mansion in red sandstone close to the burgh of Lauder in Berwickshire. The first castle here was known as Lauder Fort. This was a simple wooden structure built by Edward I as a base for his invasion of Scotland in 1296. Lauder Fort controlled the road between the Moorfoot and Lammermuir hills that led straight to Edinburgh and it changed hands several times during the Wars for Scottish Independence as a result. The original wooden fort was replaced by a stone castle around 1400 but this was captured by Lord Somerset during the Rough Wooing and converted into an artillery bastion in 1548. This in turn was re-garrisoned by a Franco-Scottish force in 1550 and dismantled soon afterwards. A fear of England was a constant in Scotland's foreign policy however, and Fort Lauder was again strengthened in 1590 to keep pace with the increasing offensive power of artillery.

The normal owners of Lauder Fort were the Maitlands of Thirlestane. Notable family members included Sir Richard 'the Blind Knight of Thirlestane' who fought against Edward I, and Sir William of Lethington, friend and confidante of Mary Queen of Scots. However the most powerful Maitland by far was John 2nd Earl and Duke of Lauderdale who governed Scotland in the absence of Charles II. The present Thirlestane Castle on the site of Lauder Fort is the result of the Duke's desire in the 1670s to build a suitably grand stately home from which to direct the government of Scotland. Thirlestane Castle is therefore a massive residence for this period, for the Duke wanted it to be as impressive as possible. The reconstruction began in 1670 under the direction of the architect Sir William Bruce who was assisted by the master mason Robert Mylne. The new faÁade with wings crowned by corner towers and a grand baroque central staircase announced to all of Lauderdale's visitors that in Scotland, he was the State. Inside Thirlestane, Bruce worked with the Duke's wife, the Countess of Dysart, to create a home of unrivalled splendour and the plaster ceilings in the staterooms easily surpass those at the royal palace of Holyrood in their scale and complexity.

The Duke of Lauderdale's moment of greatness soon passed but later generations of Maitlands had the sense and the taste to treat this great house with intelligence. Later additions were very much in sympathy with Sir William Bruce's original Jacobean plan, so that today, Thirlestane Castle is one of the finest seventeenth century palaces in Europe.

The present Drumlanrig Castle is a fine Stewart mansion but there have been several fortresses on the site in Upper Nithsdale. A castle built here around 1300 was besieged and sacked by English forces in 1375. This was the castle known to Sir James Douglas, friend of Robert the Bruce, who undertook to carry the king's embalmed heart to Jerusalem. After Bruce's death in 1329, Douglas set out on crusade but his way to the Holy Land was blocked as there had been no Christian presence there since the Fall of Acre in 1291. Consequently he ended up in Spain fighting the Moors in the cause of King Alfonso XI. Tradition says that a large force of Moors ambushed Sir James near Granada. Realizing that he could not escape, he took Bruce's heart from the casket around his neck and flung it into the advancing enemy shouting 'Forward brave heart'. The body of Douglas was found within a ring of Moors that he had killed, while Bruce's heart was returned to Melrose Abbey. The emblem of the heart can be seen throughout the current Drumlanrig Castle. The motto of the Douglass family remains 'Forward' in memory of this high moment in medieval chivalry.

The Douglasses of Drumlanrig remained steadfastly loyal to the Scottish Crown. The 2nd Earl died at Otterburn in 1388. Another Douglas acted as hostage for James I in captivity in England and was knighted at his coronation in 1424. Yet another died alongside James IV at Flodden in 1513. This reputation for loyalty to the Scottish Crown held the family in good stead when the King left for London in 1603. James VI & I and his successors needed key men that they could trust to run their now distant kingdom and the Earls of Drumlanrig fitted the bill. William Douglas, the 3rd Earl who built the present Drumlanrig was typical, serving as Privy Counsellor, Lord Justice General, Lord High Treasurer and Governor of Edinburgh Castle. In 1684 he was rewarded with the title Duke of Queensberry. He employed the master masons James Smith and Robert Mylne to build a new baronial house, probably after consulting older plans drawn up by the royal architect Sir William Bruce. The result was the magnificent pink sandstone mansion that survives today, a pinnacle in Scottish architectural history, but already considered old-fashioned by the time of its completion. The old Earl was horrified by the final costs and wrote on the cover of the building accounts book 'The Deil pike oot his een wha lookes herein'.

Floors Castle, the largest inhabited mansion in Scotland, sits above the north bank of the Tweed a little more than a mile west of Kelso in the Scottish Borders. Floors Castle was originally built for John Innes Ker, the 1st Duke of Roxburghe, in a very plain Palladian style between 1718 and 1725. The designs were drawn up by William Adam although Sir John Vanburgh may also have been consulted during its construction. The result was an unremarkable country house that despite its name had no military value. Later Dukes extended the castle on several occasions without architectural success. In the 1830s and 1840s however, Floors was extensively remodelled for the 6th Duke by the celebrated architect William Playfair who transformed the rather dull Georgian exterior into a magnificent mock-Stewart palace. Playfair drew his inspiration from elements of the Scottish vernacular architectural tradition with its emphasis upon lofty turrets and pinnacles. He was then engaged in restoring the Renaissance splendour of George Heriot's Hospital in the Old Town of Edinburgh and this clearly influenced his work at Floors. The new improved Floors was spectacular and was described by a near neighbour, Sir Walter Scott of Abbotsford, as 'a kingdom for Oberon and Titania to dwell in'.

Less than half a mile to the south of Floors on the other bank of the Tweed are the remains of the fortress of Roxburgh, the largest and strongest castle in the Borders and a key fortress in the defence of medieval Scotland. In the vast grounds of Floors, a holly tree grows on the spot where James II is thought to have died in an explosion in 1460. James was attempting to win back Roxburgh Castle when the barrel of his favourite cannon, a siege bombard called the Lion, exploded. The king was killed by the flying splinters. Little remains of the once impressive Roxburgh Castle today other than some fragments of the gatehouse, the curtain wall and its flanking towers but these are well protected by dense vegetation for much of the year and difficult to access other than in winter.

Floors Castle is home to an extensive art collection including masterpieces by Raeburn, Gainsborough, Picasso and Matisse as well as a fine collection of porcelain. The wife of the 8th Duke, the American heiress May Goelot, brought her priceless collection of seventeenth century Gobelin tapestries depicting mythological figures such as Venus and Ceres to Floors. The magnificent gates were built in 1929 to designs by the architect Reginald Fairlie. Floors remains the family home of the Duke and Duchess of Roxburghe.

In the fifteenth century, Sir Duncan Campbell moved his clan seat from its ancestral home in Loch Awe to a new location on the shores of Loch Fyne. Since the thirteenth century, the Campbell power base had been in the lands around the head of Loch Awe between Glen Dochart and the Pass of Brander. The clan memory, enshrined in songs of deeds in battle and reinforced everyday by the tilling of the landscape, rooted the men of Campbell to that distinct part of Scotland. Nevertheless Sir Duncan convinced his folk to abandon their ancient hearths and follow him to a new home at Inverary. The fact that Sir Duncan was willing to jettison centuries of tradition is testament to his Campbell ambition and vision. The Loch Awe homelands, he argued, were on the shores of an inland lake, hemmed in by narrow passes and rugged mountains. Loch Fyne was a sea loch that gave swift access to the Firth of Clyde and the Atlantic. By moving to Inverary, Clan Campbell could operate on a bigger stage.

Sir Duncan, the first laird at Inverary, epitomized the ambition of Clan Campbell. Rising to the title of Lord Campbell of Argyll, he sat in the Scottish Parliament and on the Privy Council. He encouraged his folk to work the lands of Argyll so assiduously that their output by 1600 rivalled that of more fertile areas such as Perthshire. Nor did Sir Duncan neglect the clan's military power and by the time of his death in 1453, the Campbells feared no other clan apart from the imperious Macdonalds. Nevertheless Sir Duncan was content to build a relatively modest castle at Inverary of which little record now survives. His son Colin established the surrounding burgh of Inverary in the 1470s to cement the economic power of the clan.

The present Inverary Castle is an early example of Gothic revivalism begun in 1743, at which point the Campbells not only dominated western Scotland but were one of the great aristocratic houses of Britain. The new mansion commissioned by the 3rd Duke of Argyll was the work of Roger Morris assisted by William Adam. Built of blue-green schist from Argyll, Inverary echoed Blenheim Palace as it was based around a large central tower. A rectangular plan with battlemented drum towers at each corner, Inverary has many decorative quasi-military features such as a moat, turrets and weaponry of all kinds. To ensure uninterrupted views from the castle's pseudo-Gothic windows, the entire burgh of Inverary was demolished and rebuilt half a mile to the south. Dr Johnson was an early visitor to the castle in 1773 and spoke for all subsequent guests when he remarked 'What I admire here, is the total defiance of expense'.

Dunvegan on the Isle of Skye has been the ancestral home of Clan MacLeod since the 1270s. Twenty-nine generations of clan chief have owned Dunvegan, giving the castle a strong claim to be the oldest residence in Britain continuously occupied by the same family. Part of the reason for this continuity of ownership stems from Dunvegan's impregnability. Surrounded on three sides by cliffs and Loch Dunvegan, the fortress sits on a rocky promontory within a curtain wall. For much of Dunvegan's history, the only way into the castle in times of crisis was through its northern sea-gate allowing it to be supplied throughout the longest siege. A permanent stone bridge across the castle ditch to the mainland of Skye was only built in 1748. The fourteenth century square keep and sixteenth century Fairy Tower were badly affected by the unadventurous remodelling of the castle in the 1840s which gives it its present grim appearance.

The court of Chief MacLeod at Dunvegan Castle was at the heart of the unique way of life that existed upon Skye before the nineteenth century. The Piper's Gallery honours the memory of Chief Alastair Crotach who founded the College of Pipers for the MacCrimmons, the hereditary pipers to the clan chief. The Dunvegan Cup of Irish origin held within the castle is a reminder that Hebridean chiefs with their birlinns or galleys could meddle in Hibernian as well as Caledonian affairs. Lavish feasting in the castle's hall was a way of showering largesse upon his warriors and holding their loyalty. When the chief wanted to impress a Lowland visitor, he could always dine upon MacLeod's Tables, the two flat-topped mountains that dominate the landscape above the castle.

Clan MacLeod turned out in full to support Charles II in his bid for the Crown in 1650. Over seven hundred clansmen were killed at the Battle of Worcester the following year. This devastating loss had a silver lining for it allowed the MacLeods to sit out the Jacobite Risings of 1689 and 1715, excused by their neighbours who understood their need to replenish their manpower. The 25th chief of the clan earned a special place in Highland hearts during the potato famine of 1847. While other Highland landowners used the famine to clear their small tenants from the land, Macleod bankrupted himself trying to provide for his hungry people. He ended up having to take a post as a clerk to earn a living while renting the castle to clear his debts. He was only able to return to his beloved Dunvegan as an old man.

Thanks to William Shakespeare, the name of Glamis Castle is forever linked to Macbeth. The murder of the sleeping King Duncan by the Thane of Glamis was a figment of the bard's imagination, but the real eleventh century Macbeth would have known Glamis for it was a celebrated shrine to St Fergus as far back as 700 AD and the surrounding area was a hunting ground for the kings of Alba. One medieval king did die at Glamis, but this was Malcolm II, injured at the Battle of Hunter's Hill in 1034 and carried to Glamis where he passed away. Shakespeare did do some research into the history of the area however, possibly staying at Glamis en route to Aberdeen in 1599.

The recorded history of Glamis Castle begins with a grant of land by Robert II to John Lyon who promptly married the king's daughter and received a knighthood in return. In due course John rose to be Chancellor of Scotland. The second laird of Glamis also married a Stewart princess and began building a fine keep in the fourteenth century, the core of the present castle.

Due to the crackdown by James V on his nobility, the lords of Glamis lost their estates. James was so taken with this elegant fortalice in the rich Angus landscape that he moved the Court to Glamis for part of each year between 1537 to 1542. The young 7th laird regained the castle when his royal enemy died after the Battle of Solway Moss but he found the castle stripped of its valuables by the rapacious Stewart courtiers. Twenty years later, Mary Queen of Scots, who was thought to have felt guilty about her vindictive father's actions, helped make good the fortunes of Lord Glamis and enjoyed a happy visit to the castle in 1562. In 1606 the Lords of Glamis were raised to the Earldom of Kinghorne, though their title eventually became Earl of Kinghorne and Strathmore. During the sixteenth and seventeenth centuries, Glamis developed into a baronial mansion as much as a place of defence, with most of the outer fortifications of the castle being demolished to make way for formal baroque gardens and sculpture walks.

Glamis is reputedly the most haunted castle in Britain. One of its ghosts is Janet Douglas, the widow of the 6th Lord Glamis, who was imprisoned and burned as a witch by James V. Its most famous spectre is Beardie who unwittingly played cards with the devil, lost his soul and now lives in a secret room within the castle. Other Glamis ghosts include Jack the Runner and the weeping boy, the first and possibly only black ghost in Scotland.

Culzean castle on the Ayrshire coast is a masterpiece of the Scottish Gothic Revival. Sir Thomas Kennedy who inherited the title of Earl of Cassilis in 1762 had been on the Grand Tour and had been impressed not only by the classical grandeur of Rome but by the many fine medieval buildings throughout the continent. Thomas had already inherited the Kennedy castle of Culzean about ten miles south of Ayr and felt that its dramatic cliff-top location, with views across the Firth of Clyde to Arran and the Mull of Kintyre, was the perfect site for a new family seat. Between 1762 and 1775, Sir Thomas repaired the old castle and added a new wing. His successor, David 10th Earl Cassilis also decided to live at Culzean Castle but planned far greater changes. He commissioned Robert Adam to build one of the finest and grandest mansions in the kingdom, bankrupting himself in the process. The result was an unparalleled romantic fantasy on the outside and a perfect neo-classical Adam Georgian home within. Its design and execution rank with the finest Enlightenment architecture anywhere in Europe. The strain of this massive undertaking affected both the artist and patron however. Adam wore himself out travelling between London and Ayrshire and died of an ignored stomach haemorrhage in 1795. The penniless Earl of Cassilis died of worry later the same year.

The first Culzean castle had been a humble keep built to protect the lands of the local Kennedy family. Although close to Central Scotland, parts of Ayrshire had a reputation for independence and lawlessness. The old Culzean castle sat above a coast honeycombed with caverns. It was a natural landscape for smuggling and the medieval Kennedys probably both connived at, and participated in, that ancient trade.

Castles have been the homes of warlords since the early Middle Ages so the lifetime gift of the top apartments at Culzean Castle to General Dwight Eisenhower in 1945 was an appropriate gesture. Returning to Culzean as President of the USA in the 1950s, the castle was converted into the 'Scottish White House' complete with all the Cold War trappings.

As befits a mansion on this scale, Culzean has a retinue of ghosts. A spectral piper announces forthcoming marriages within the Kennedy clan while a female ghost has the good sense to dress appropriately in a ball gown. A third apparition is that of a knight who abducted an heiress and carried her to Culzean, only to be stabbed to death by the woman who used his own dirk for the deed.

Dunrobin Castle, on a rocky spur a mile along the coast from Golspie in Sutherland, will always be remembered as the fairy tale castle built upon the nightmare of the Highland Clearances. Although the present appearance of the castle is defined by its nineteenth century Franco-Scottish Gothic embellishments, Dunrobin is an old fortress with a long history. The first knight here was Freskin de Moravia, a Norman baron who fought for David I and William the Lion in the re-conquest of the northern territories. One of Freskin's grandsons inherited the Earldom of Sutherland in 1235 which passed in time to the Gordons.

Dunrobin is the largest castle in the northern Highlands. Some elements of the castle are thought to date back to the time of William, the 3rd Earl in the 1320s, while a keep was added in 1401. Although some military features are still apparent, such as the fine iron yett, the original defensive nature of the structure has been well masked by later re-modelling in the 1840s and again in 1915. Dunrobin's similarity to a Loire chateau derives from the work of the Gothic Revivalist Sir Charles Barry between 1845 and 1851. At Dunrobin he created a memorable multi-turreted fantasy in the fake baronial style known as 'Balmorality'.

Dunrobin Castle was witness to one of the worst misunderstandings in Scottish history. In April 1746 George Mackenzie, the Jacobite 3rd Earl of Cromartie, was led to believe by a messenger that the Hanoverians had been defeated at Culloden. Without waiting to confirm the news, the Earl rounded up his men and siezed Dunrobin Castle in the name of Charles Edward Stewart. As the real news from Culloden filtered north, the Earl found himself surrounded by the Sutherland militia and was eventually captured in the apartment at Dunrobin still known today as the Cromartie Room.

Dunrobin Castle will always be associated with Elizabeth Gordon, the nineteenth century Countess of Sutherland who married the exceptionally wealthy Marquis of Stafford in 1785 and set out to 'improve' her Highland estates. Although the Staffords built 450 miles of new road in Sutherland and encouraged new tenants to bring over 200,000 sheep into the county, they are remembered for the brutal clearances of Strathnaver. Their hated factor Patrick Sellar despised the local Gaelic folk, believing them to be lazy and an obstacle to progress. The Clearances on the Sutherland estates were amongst the most oppressive as a result. Two years after 1814, remembered as 'The Year of the Burnings', Sellar was in fact tried for murder and fire-raising.

In the Middle Ages, a Drummond castle stood on this site between Ballater and Braemar, but by 1600 the castle and estate of Balmoral lay within the vast lands of the Earl of Mar. In the seventeenth and eighteenth centuries, Balmoral passed to the Farquharsons of Inverey and then to the Earl of Fife until in the 1830s it became the home of Sir Robert Gordon, brother of the Prime Minister, the Earl of Aberdeen. Only one image of this earlier Balmoral Castle survives, luckily captured by the pioneering photographer George Washington Wilson shortly before the castle's demolition in 1856. The photograph reveals an early battlemented square keep with a fine pepper-pot corner tower, upstaged by Georgian and Gothic Revival extensions.

This was the castle that Victoria and Albert leased in 1848. The royal couple had been looking for a permanent summer home in Scotland but without success. Then Prince Albert investigated the meteorological records and found that Deeside was drier than most other parts of the Highlands, which appealed to his advancing rheumatism. The rolling hills of Deeside also reminded him of his native Thuringia. For her part, Victoria was taken with the views of Lochnagar to the south west of the castle. She knew Lord Byron's poem 'Dark Lochnagar' and had doubtless heard Beethoven's arrangement of Byron's romantic hymn to this majestic mountain. The Saxe-Coburgs purchased Balmoral in 1852 but soon realized that it was too small for their needs.

Albert commissioned the Aberdeen architect William Smith to work with him on planning a new royal palace at a site about eighty yards east of the old castle. Victoria laid the foundation stone in September 1853 on top of a time capsule containing coins and a signed parchment. When the royal family arrived at Balmoral for its summer holiday in August 1857, not a single stone of the old castle could be seen.

The new palace, capable of holding over 120 guests and court functionaries, was constructed in the Scots Baronial style using white granite from nearby Glen Gelder. The exterior of Balmoral contained every architectural device that suggested a medieval fortress such as machiolation, tourelles and a battlemented Stewart tower but this decoration only just masked the reality of Balmoral as a rationally planned country house with two main blocks, one for guests and the other for service functions. The new Highland palace served its purpose well for Balmoral Castle could easily accommodate Victoria's growing family, as well as the entourage of ministers and secretaries needed for the smooth running of the state during the monarch's absence from London. So devoted was the Queen to Balmoral and Deeside that the ruler of the world's largest Empire regularly spent up to one third of every year in this castellated Highland idyll.

Bailey outer wall and courtyard of a castle, usually housing service and storage areas

Ballistae Originally a large Roman crossbow, periodically 're-invented' throughout the medieval period

Barbican projecting tower over the gate of a castle or other key defensive point in a wall

Bartizan correctly a gallery projecting outwards from a castle wall face but often used in Scotland to mean a corbelled corner turret

Barmkin in Scotland usually applied to a low battlemented wall round a castle

Battering inward sloping of castle walls to better absorb the force of artillery shot

Birlinn shallow-draught galleys used by medieval Highland clans, derived from Norse longships

Bombard large bore siege cannon of the late medieval period circa 1300 -1450

Broch Iron Age dry-built circular towers found throughout northern Scotland

Caponier covered gun passage flanking a ditch or trench

Castellan governor or captain in charge of a castle

Constable in medieval Scotland, an officer charged with holding a castle and keeping the law

Crenellation the indentation along the top of a castle wall commonly called battlements

Donjon usually the largest tower or innermost keep of a castle

Embrasure opening in a wall that widens from within so that a gun can be fired outwards at varying angles. See gun loops

Enceinte enclosure or courtyard encircled by a high castle wall

Enfilade to fire from within a castle along the length of a section of castle wall

Fortalice small fortified place

Fosse sunken ditch or moat

Gallowglass distinctive Irish warriors of the late medieval-early modern period

Gun loops See embrasures

Keep central or strongest tower of a castle

Machiolation openings between corbels high on a castle wall from which objects, boiling water or boiling sand can be dropped onto assailants

Mangonel medieval siege engine for throwing stones, usually by a spoon-tipping action

Merk Scots mark worth 13s 4d in Scots coinage or 13 and a half Sterling pennies

Mormaer high ranking nobleman in pre-feudal Celtic Scotland

Moss-trooper derogative term used for royalist irregulars in the 1640s and 1650s

Motte earth mound surmounted by a wooden tower in the period 1050 - 1150

Ogee continuous double curved shape sometime used to top a turret

Palisade thick fence made of pales or stakes

Parapet fortification, usually stone, designed to protect defenders from enemy observation and fire

Peel originally a palisade but in Scotland also used for a small fortification

Postern small castle entrance usually in a rear or covered position, used for surprise sallies against the attackers. Sometimes called sally ports.

Ravelin outer fortification with two faces meeting at a salient angle, usually built to deliver forward artillery fire

Tourelle small circular turret in a French Renaissance style

Trebuchet medieval siege engine casting stones through the sudden release of weight at one end of a pendulum

Yett thick iron grille protecting a doorway